365 Little Blasts of Love

Daily Doses of Uncensored Wisdom to Radically Shift Your Life

AMY L. FIEDLER

365 Little Blasts of Love

Copyright © 2016 by Amy L. Fiedler/Winky Boo, LLC

All rights reserved. No part of this book may be reproduced, scanned, or distributed in any printed or electronic form without permission.

Cover art © Michael Zosh
www.michaelzosh.com

Photography © Corie
www.artbycorie.com

Interior design by Michael Zosh

ISBN-13: 978-1530208166
ISBN-10: 1530208165

For more, visit www.amythelifecoach.com
or email NJSelfHelp@gmail.com

For Little Amy,

You are never alone.

You will never be alone.

Introduction

For a very long time in my life, I felt lost, forgotten, and sad. I was confused on why I was even here...like alive on Earth. I used to think about this stuff when I was younger in my early teens, and it seemed to escalate as the years went on. All through my teenage years and twenties I was on a rollercoaster of emotions. We could only call it the rollercoaster of doom. I was anxious, insecure, sad, stressed, angry, and depressed. Not 'hypothetically' depressed; a therapist diagnosed me as depressed. Mind you 'depression' was just one item on the list of "problems" I was labeled. I was also told I had anxiety and OCD.

So I thought I was crazy. That felt and sounded crazy, and well, when you've seen a psychiatrist as a teen, there wasn't another word to use to describe how I felt. The point is counseling, therapy, and pills only made me feel lonelier. I was handed the workbook they give to every person that comes in, then listened to a man tell me it was all my parent's fault and, "Would they be willing to come in for a session?"

No. No, they would not.

I eventually stopped going and ended up in a psychic's shop one day. After she had given me a reading (which was spot on in case you were wondering), I burst into tears and covered my face. She sternly yet in a motherly way told me to sit up, wipe my eyes, and knock it off. She said I can help you. I couldn't afford her, so she took me under her wing and offered me a job in exchange for help. I clearly see now what God was doing behind the scenes. Had I known just ten years later I'd be spiritually working with people to guide and heal their inner wounds, then at the time I might not have felt so.... crazy.

See we never know what God has in store. It'd be nice if we did sometimes but wouldn't that take all the fun and storytelling out of living! I mean for starters.... you wouldn't have this delicate yet profound intro into my book.

Hell... you might not even have had the book had I already known what God was doing back in the day.

And before you continue reading further I want to make this clear...the name GOD is interchangeable with Universe/Source/Spirit/The Dude Upstairs/ Higher Self or whatever other name resonates most with you. I connect with the name God, but I will often use other terms to replace it – either way this is by no means about a name or title or any religion. It's not about religion at all because recognizing a GOD is not a religious act.

It's about a connection with yourself.

It took me quite some time to realize that "God" is merely a name for our higher self. That it's IN me. It's the smarter version of us. Yes... there's one of those. It lives inside of you, and this "body" or human shell of yours just houses it.

So you have your body and inside you have all sorts of organs and shit but I'm no doctor and what I want you to connect with is beyond those things – it surpasses a name because I am by no means religious.

God is IN you and around you. This dude gets an awful stigma, but you see GOD (your higher self) is all over the damn place and he/she/it has nothing to do with dangling on a cross or referencing a verse in The Bible. Which, although fascinating and theological, reflective and full of divine experiences, is a man-made book that was written by humans who are merely shells of God. It's a book about human life with spiritual sight. Kind of like this book. Well...exactly like this book. You get the point.

God is in you and me. He's in the world and all around us. IT connects us all, and it has infinite wisdom because it is energy (i.e., Energy SOURCE.... are you following me now?).

This is all clicking for you isn't it!

Simply put: God is a higher power and that higher power is in you and everyone and everything.

So when you look at another, you see yourself. When you talk to another, you are talking to yourself. This world is a giant mirror reflecting you to you. The purpose it serves is to bring you closer to yourself; to teach you about yourself; to help you understand your purpose here and love every single thing you learn…. the good, the bad and even the ugly.

So what are you about to dive into and how is it going to help you?

A few years ago I was running a business of mine. I thought it was my passion. I had gone to college and studied photography and digital art and upon graduating, I went on to have some amazing jobs in the art and fashion world. Keep in mind I was still working with, and for, on occasion my dear psychic from high school until the present. So throughout everything I am about to share, I was still in the midst of this spiritual arena I felt drawn to but had no idea why.

I'm not big on name-dropping as I genuinely have a fear of not being humble enough if I succeed too much (I'm working on it) so we'll keep this brief. I had some high profile gigs post-college and low profile gigs. I worked for and with celebrities in the photography and fashion world. Names you've heard of and fully recognize to this day. I experienced a lot and truly had a blast learning my way around NYC and the fashion styling world while assisting amazing wardrobe stylists, working on huge photoshoots, music videos, movies, television shows and more.

I thought this was my dream. I had always loved fashion and was naturally good at it. It was good for the time I was at in my life. I had the freedom I wanted, a "big girl job" in my opinion and it was quite fabulous in some aspects…at least to others. So I could feed my ego even though as I mentioned above I'm not a big bragger. I tend to keep important and exciting things super close to my heart. I've learned to be proud of myself more now and share my journey…all pieces of it (hence this whole book thing).

Let me get to the point: This was all amazing stuff, and I was making great money, but it wasn't fulfilling. I always felt like I was searching for more. I felt like a piece of me was missing from all of this in a big way but I had no idea what it was.

As time went on, I got less and less excited about traveling for photo shoots at weird hours of the day. I got tired of thinking about the long commute and then having to drive in and around the city from showroom to showroom. I was exhausted and bored with it. So right then and there I should have recognized the power of the law of attraction in my life because the minute I decided I was over it…. God intervened to help me out.

I said no to having to travel into the city for work one time and the next thing I knew I was old news in the assistant styling world. You say no and they find someone who says yes.

It wasn't because I was bad at my job… I was amazing. I was even encouraged to move to the city so I could get more gigs but it wasn't where I desired to be. So I decided internally, and God worked externally to rearrange shit in my favor.

Cut to months later and I decide I'll start a clothing company. This is the business I mentioned earlier that I thought was my passion. I wanted only to answer to myself, and since I knew I was good at fashion, I thought this was the way.

I named the company using nicknames my grandfather had given me and my siblings and had my dear friend from college who is a master at illustration help me create the most amazing logo in the world. Yes, I will label it that because in the end, after all was said and done, I still look at that name and logo and smile.

I called it Winky Boo thanks to my PopPop and his creative play on words he used for nicknames…or perhaps it was his beer talking but either way… Casper you're still a genius. No, really, that's his name. Even though he has long since passed on and well, you get the reference he's quite magical, alive, and in spirit.

I didn't have money to start a clothing company, and God intervened once more. This is important, and I almost left it out of the book because who likes long intros. Now I get it. They're necessary for a backstory. During this time of me figuring out I wanted to start my own business I was working as a nanny for my psychic. One evening I was home with her father and three of the kids and her father yelled to me saying he needed help taking his blood pressure.

I helped him take it, and he explained to me he wasn't feeling well and had chest pain. I read the numbers and having grown up with a mother in medicine I knew what was happening. I grabbed the kids and put him in the car because her father and I agreed we didn't have time to dial 911 and wait. He was having a heart attack. I nervously got him to the hospital where his wife was waiting to meet him. Had we not left the house when we did, the doctor said, "if he arrived 1 minute later; he would be dead."

So I saved a man's life. That was overwhelming and frightening. Meanwhile, I turned right back around upon dropping him off to drive the kids back home. I got lost because I was shook up and I ended up in a car accident. My car got totaled. The kids were safe. I fractured my collarbone. This was God.

See often people wonder why bad things happen to good people. I frequently get asked how I could possibly begin to spiritually explain bad things in life, like death or tragic events, or even car accidents. Everything "bad" is actually good. That's exactly what I tell them. It's only our limited human perception labeling it bad but in spiritual truth there are no labels, only love is real.

Yes, my car got totaled AFTER I saved a man's life. Yes, I was the only one who got injured out of everyone involved. Yes, this was a car I had paid for in cash proudly with money I inherited years prior – it was my first ever large purchase of my life.

It was gone; I was hurt, but God was working. It was all good.

It needed to happen. It had to happen. That insurance money for my car, I creatively used to invest in my clothing business and chose to finance a car instead. See God provides and you decide! You can either take the inspired action or sit on it. I chose to take it. Nothing bad is actually bad if we choose not to label it as such.

Little did I know my life would come full circle after having prepared me using all these other events. I now help people find the light, and some say, "save their life." I help them comfort the inner child within through the experience I had helping to raise 7 actual children. I provide them the safe space and comfort I never could find until I met my psychic to be themselves. I explain how everything and everyone in their life is actually helping them.... after having gone through and learned that everything we experience is a reflection from within. I remind them of who they really are so they don't have to take the long road searching out there. And I help them understand the shit they feel that I never understood until I took all these other amazing detours leading me right back home to who I was always meant to be.

I'll save you the analysis of this part of my journey by simply saying after thousands of dollars invested in my clothing business, with little to no profit to show for it after six years... I had had enough. I didn't know how to be done, but I couldn't even look at the clothing I had created anymore. Truly the only thing holding me there was that I had a Registered Trademark of the name Winky Boo that during the process of registering it, I had to battle it out in court with a rather large boutique with a not-so-similar name. Why did this keep me holding on? Because of course it was another proud accomplishment of my own that I did all by myself that I had given me zero credit for.

I fought for a trademark with no actual trademark or legal experience, and I won. I won against a really large company who had an entire law firm representing them. Amy vs. Giant Law Firm. Google and innate divine wisdom vs. law school. And I won. That's a big feat that, once again, I shrugged off and moved on from and then when it came down to following my heart with my business... I was holding onto an accomplishment simply because I never acknowledged it.

Lesson: Take time to honor your accomplishments. It's more important than you think to give yourself the credit of anything and everything you've done in your life. The big stuff and the small stuff.

I had been trying to force a path that wasn't me for long enough. There was no depth. I couldn't find my sweet spot in the fashion world when it came to all parts of me. I couldn't find a way to incorporate ALL of me into what I was doing. While sitting one day with a notebook, I decided to write down everything that I loved that made me, me. I wrote everything from the colors I liked to the things that interested me like helping people and writing. As days passed and pages of my notebook filled, it got more detailed and clear. I started writing about how people always have asked me for help, and I'm the pillar of strength for those around me... even when I feel weak. Now I'm weeks into journaling my interests and thoughts out, and I suddenly say to myself, "I should be a life coach."

No really... it happened just like that. No one told me. No one suggested it. No one guided me there. It just clicked and at the time, I didn't even know if there was such a thing. I had to sit down and Google if this profession existed. Lo and behold it did and here we are.

So I donated all the clothing remaining in stock from my clothing company because I just wanted it gone and out of my room. I was tired of staring at boxes of t-shirts, and I didn't care about the money. I wanted to move on so badly I left it all behind.

With that said, here we are.

So what's an affirmation and why did I start writing them?

They weren't something I personally used or practiced, but as I was transitioning my business from clothing over to coaching, I started writing on my blog on my clothing company website every day. I would write my thoughts or something inspirational.

Suddenly it began to transform into a daily thought with a bit of guidance that I needed a name for and while looking up what that might be I find the word affirmation.

Affirmations are a declaration, a statement, or a proclamation that provides emotional support or encouragement. It's a process of positively affirming something we believe we want to manifest (create). When I read about them, I realized I was writing these without really knowing I was doing so. So I started labeling them daily affirmations on my blog, and I committed to writing one daily mostly for myself at the time as it helped me, guided me and inspired me. Little did I know it would turn into something so much larger that would impact thousands of people.

I began sharing them on my social media pages from Facebook to Twitter to LinkedIn, and I suddenly had a following. Complete strangers were messaging me saying how young and wise I was. They'd tell me how much my words impacted them that day or how one thought of mine changed their entire perception of something in their life.

I was blown away.

I had no idea that something I just simply enjoyed doing would impact others in such a great way. I had no idea because I had made life and work so hard up until this point. It was time to start making it easy on myself. It was time for a fresh new beginning full of everything I love. So I wrote an affirmation every single day for two years straight never missing a day.

I never missed a day even when I was sick, sad, lonely or broken hearted. I used it as a way to get through, speak to God, heal, understand and release. I had no idea at the time I was helping others heal, learn, and grow while I preached.

Now I understand. I understand that everything you see and experience is a reflection of your inner condition. It always comes back to this. It always comes back to you. It takes a brave soul to look themselves in the mirror and say, "Yes that was me, I did it." But you know what...it's true. It's always you. It's never about them...it's always about you on the inside...how you're feeling towards yourself in each moment and situation you encounter. If you can get right with you and not worry what others do...I promise you that you will master this peaceful existence as God intended.

Life is just a puzzle with all these other people and experiences as the pieces that fit together to show you who you are and what you're made of.

You don't need to be good at puzzles to navigate life.... you just need to be good with yourself.

How to Use This Book

This part is crucial so pay close attention. This is not your average book. Nor is it the type of book you pick up once, read through, and put back on the shelf never to return again.

This book is one you use; you utilize, lean on, and turn to.

Hell… make notes and highlight the shit out of it will ya! That's how you know it's a good book.

This book is full of magic, and it contains miracles because it speaks to your soul. I know this because I speak to your soul. My friend calls me the Soul Whisperer. When I sit down with a client or when I'm out in the real world and roaming the supermarket, souls are speaking to me. I know things without knowing how I know them. I receive messages without knowing how they come through. I don't need to know you to know what your soul is calling home for you because when it comes to spiritual truth, we are one.

We are connected. You and I and that dude to your left. Ok so there's no dude, that's fine, but one may cross your path pretty soon.

The point is, there are 365 affirmations here. There is one for every single day of the year because I didn't stop writing which means your soul didn't stop speaking.

You may not understand now but in time, you will. Reading this book will provide you guidance, wisdom, revelation, clarification, and confirmation for whatever is burning in your soul. Synchronicities will unfold throughout your day. You will experience miracles. You will grow. You will heal. You will learn. You will remember. You will reclaim your power. You will feel fearless and inspired. You will change. You will glow. You will get in the flow. And you will know that you were led to this book to enhance your mind, body, and soul.
So here's how you can use this book.

Close the book now.

Go ahead... close it, Well, after you read the rest of my instructions.

Close the book and place your hand on top of the cover. I don't care what hand just pick a hand and put it on the damn cover.

Now close your eyes and repeat after me:

> Dear (God/Universe/Source).
> I need some guidance today.
> I want you to show me the way.
> Please light the way and turn me to the exact page that will heal my soul and put a smile on my face.
> Give me my little blast of love today!
> Amen

Now open the book at random. Whatever page you land on you need.
Or I've given you another option...

You may read from front to back per usual, but no matter which way you choose to read this book, it will sync up with your life. Even if you don't think so, it WILL. Even if you miss a week of reading and come back to it, it will sync up with your life.

That means if you're reading it, you needed it. Even if you didn't think you did at the time (it will click later, it always does, I promise).
Now one more thing...

When you are done reading your affirmation each day, as you close the book say this:

> Thank you.

Don't worry, it knows who you're speaking to and so do you, whether you consciously choose to realize it or not.

The heart always knows the truth because the truth is always simple.
Ok, now it's time you shut the book and start your journey.

Don't worry though it's all inward and it's all beautiful. It's all always helping to heal you.

Thank you for letting my soul speak to you.

Glossary

There are some key terms that I'd like to reference so you can fully understand their meaning.

Affirmation: A positive statement that provides emotional support, encouragement, and empowerment.

Ego: The human version of you. The jaded, scared, hurt, sad, fearful part of who you are that is limited and only knows fear. Other synonyms: negative energy, negativity, Devil.

God: The spirit version of you. The wiser part of your being that is limitless and only knows love. Other synonyms: spirit, source, universe, positive energy, positivity, higher self.

"I AM": A way of referencing the God within you; your higher self. It's a powerful way to speak to your soul. Speaking the words, "I AM" helps you bypass your ego instantly.

Law of Attraction: The idea that "like attracts like". Positive thoughts and energy attract positive experiences, and negative thoughts and energy attract negative experiences. Also referred to as the Law of Vibration.

Spirituality: The connection between yourself and the universe. The sacred act of getting to know yourself in the midst of this world we live in. A journey within.

Synchronicity: Coined by psychiatrist Carl Jung, it means that events have "meaningful coincidences". i.e.: Everything happens for a reason. There are no coincidences. Everything always connects.

Miracle: A shift in perception from fear to love. A correction that undoes error in your thinking to remind you anything fearful is false because only love is real.

Let's begin your journey...

Today's Daily Affirmation is:

What I think, I create.

Your thoughts are powerful things. They stem from things you once experienced. That's right! You literally replay old sh*t in your mind all day, every day, that is unless you choose otherwise. You can choose to think a new thought at any point in your day; the problem is we find it hard to break our old story and tell a new one.

So here's what I guide clients to do: Choose what feels good. You only want to experience what is going to feel good so only choose the thoughts that feel good and that will be exactly what unfolds into your reality.

Today's Daily Affirmation is:

I focus on what is now. I live in the present.

You ever get overwhelmed by what is coming next? Future-tripping is what we lovingly call that – where we sit dwelling anxiously in the future that has yet to exist. Guess what? The present moment is what creates the future. That's right! Right now is what is determining what is next so if you're not focused on now and only worried about what might unfold, you're only creating more worry for your future.

But what if you stayed calm and at ease right now knowing that all is well? What if you really paid attention to what is around you in THIS very moment and smiled and said, "Thank You"? Then what? Then what unfolds next will be calm and peaceful too. What happens next will feel good because you doll, feel good RIGHT NOW. This moment creates the next moment and so on and so forth.

If you find it hard to stay in THIS moment, that's because you fear that by not worrying or thinking about the future, you're releasing control over it. Just the opposite my darling…. when you trust that everything is happening for your good and let go of all the worries and focus on being happy now – you gain even more power and control over what happens next than if you were to worry. Get it? When you are at peace, you have MORE power.

Today's Daily Affirmation is:

I am confident. I am beautiful. I deserve happiness and love.

Today I want you to focus on yourself. It's ok to be a little **selfish** once in a while. Focus on what you love about yourself and *block out* any negativity that creeps in trying to bring you down. The world will always descend on us (you'll hear me say that a lot). It's kind of the world's job by nature to test us with its happenings and other humans.

Naturally, you can get sucked into feeling like you're caught up in a whirlwind of stuff and things and emotions and fear and guilt, etc. This is why constantly coming back to your CENTER and focusing on YOU is important. What is IN you reflects around you. It's selfless to focus on yourself because then your experience and the humans you encounter will be that of peace if you're at peace. If you're all up in turmoil, that'll reflect all around, and that is NO way to live…trust me; I've been there.

So by honoring yourself and your needs, you fill up on your own love and allow that to expand all around you. The minute negative thoughts come into your mind, repeat this affirmation to yourself in your head or out loud and watch how it works.

Today's Daily Affirmation is:

I will not let anyone or anything control my emotions. Only I have control over my emotions.

I hope the last three days were a bit easier for you to get through now that you have somewhere to turn every day for some <u>strength, guidance, and wisdom</u>. Each day is a *fresh start* – let go of yesterday, its troubles, its fears, its doubts and worries and face today with a *clear mind and passion* in your heart.

Today you get to choose again. If you fell off the positive path yesterday – no sweat – today, you have the power to jump back on. You have that power any second of any day. You never have to wait for a new day dolls. The power is ALL in your mind, and you can shift that sh*t at any time you desire. The point of life is to be able to become so self-aware of our own bullsh*t that we can call ourselves out, forgive ourselves for it, laugh at it, and shift back to where we desire to go. Knowing yourself is what leads to wisdom. Knowing yourself so damn well that nothing can throw you off course, but realizing IF it does, that's cool because you have the power to get back on at any moment you choose.

Today's Daily Affirmation is:

I see the positive in all that is around me today.

Everything happening is happening FOR you. It has only been placed in your path for the purpose of growing you, healing you, and preparing you for what you desire to come. You see, you asked for something. You desire something in your heart, and when you ask for it, God and the entire Universe full of positive forces conspire together to deliver it to you.

Even if it looks bad, it's good. It's only "bad" because of how you're programmed to perceive it. You've been preprogrammed by this human world, but the spiritual world doesn't follow the same rules, so you need to reprogram your brain to understand its workings and how they're benefiting you…always and forever.

Today's Daily Affirmation is:

I acknowledge that I am one-of-a-kind and I have a lot to offer this world.

You, my dear, are a light this world has never seen before. You were created so unique with a divine purpose that can only shine through if you allow it to. That means stop comparing yourself to what others do! What you see in them is in you.

That means they are a reflection that is there to show you just how special you are. This world is a mirror and the people in it are put here to reflect for you the good, the bad, and the ugly that all resides inside of you. But here's the thing…that bad sh*t – it's just an old story you picked up along the way. The bad sh*t never serves you. It dims your sparkle and keeps you small and powerless. By staying small and powerless this world and the people meant to heal from your unique light will remain in darkness too. Rise up and recognize your purpose is to help heal the world. But first, you must heal you!

Today's Daily Affirmation is:

I am confident I will succeed in all things I put my mind to.

We ebb and flow in life. Life is always going to be a series of hills and valleys – you might be hanging in the valley now, but eventually you'll make it up the hill. Keep in mind you're never going to contently sit in one spot. We go through ups and downs for reasons – be it to learn, to be taught patience, or other important lessons in life. So basically...like the waves, we ebb and flow for a purpose...a reason and that reason is benefiting you as we've already learned.

It may NOT LOOK like it's benefiting you but change your mind about what you see and what you see will change. Believing that it's all working out for you always is the definition of faith. Believing in what you know but have yet to see.

For a long time, I never understood people having faith but then I put it to the test for several years. I felt like I had pitched a tent in the damn valley and all signs directing God on how to find me went missing. I truly believed this, but it didn't feel good. So my thoughts were making me not feel good, and I knew that to change my circumstances I had to change my thoughts now. I couldn't wait for the circumstances to change first because that's not the way energy works.

Today's Daily Affirmation is:

I acknowledge that life can change in a split second. My best blessings come when I least expect them to.

Sometimes we look at what's happening in our life and get upset at how much further we feel we need to go to get to where we desire to be. But get this - change happens in an instant. And even better (though we often forget), it happens when you least expect it.

Change is good. Without it, nothing good would ever happen. And when we're in a good place, change is still good, because without it nothing BETTER can happen. It serves a purpose. It happens daily. The idea of time is irrelevant because time is not of the divine. God's time is not OUR time.

So if you can take your mind off of the idea that it might take "time" to get to where you desire to be and start believing that all it takes is your MIND catching up to your divine reality…. you will see miracles unfold instantly! Go ahead, try it…you'll see what I mean.

Today's Daily Affirmation is:

I will live in the moment.

We all have a habit of looking ahead to the *future* and wondering what it will bring. It's nice to daydream at times but to get caught up in it can only bring your spirit down – especially if your present moment isn't anything like what you hope your future will be. Today I want you to **focus** on living in the present, **enjoying what is happening around you every second of today because today is what is creating your future**. That's how energy works! What you focus on expands. Right now, focus on feeling good and your future will feel good too.

Today's Daily Affirmation is:

I will satisfy my needs today. I will do only what brings me happiness.

We've been taught backward. We've been told that caring for ourselves first is wrong. I was always taught to put others before myself and boy did that f&ck me up down the road when I learned it was supposed to be the other way around. No wonder I always felt walked all over.

We can only learn from the level we're at. Meaning our teachers are all only doing the best they can. Those "teachers" are anyone from your very own parents to grandparents to neighbors, friends, and siblings. Even the stranger at the store is a spiritual teacher for your soul. Otherwise, they wouldn't be in your existence...but once more...they all can only teach from the level they're at.

So were you taught backward too? Were you told to put you last? Because I'm here to tell you to put you first. Honoring your needs, wants, and desires FIRST is what will teach others to honor and value you too. It also helps them elevate in their own life and grow. As you grow, they grow. That's how this sh*t works. So today ask yourself, "What do I need" before you do anything, and honor it. Put you first. Give to you and as you fill up your cup – love will overflow all around you!

Today's Daily Affirmation is:

I know my truth.

Don't let anyone talk you out of what you know you're capable of doing. **Know your own worth** and know your truth. Just because another says it, doesn't make it true. You know that voice deep down inside you? **Trust it, believe it, and follow it, wholeheartedly**.

Today's Daily Affirmation is:

I will give thanks for the things I do have and trust that the things I need or want will arrive in due time.

Today is a good time to *focus on your blessings*. By blessings I mean, what do you have in your life that is good, that is wonderful, that is right? You're reading this so obviously you woke up this morning – that's a blessing. Do you have a computer or a roof over your head – more blessings! Remember, **the things you take for granted, someone else is praying for.**

Today's Daily Affirmation is:

I believe in myself. I will succeed. All that I need is already in me.

Not everyone is going to support you or your dreams. Your dreams are just that – **YOUR DREAMS**. You will find few people that truly want to see you do good in the world and *then you will find many people who want to see you do good, but never better than them*. Stay focused and don't let **"dream killers"** put a damper on your excitement for the future.

Today's Daily Affirmation is:

I know the Universe is working in my favor. I deserve all of the great things that I am creating and manifesting.

Life is full of *infinite possibilities*. You can do anything you want to do and be anything you want to be. **Don't allow others to place restrictions on your dreams**. Place your desires out into the Universe and *have faith in yourself*.

Today's Daily Affirmation is:

I will not give up. I was given today for a reason.

Wake up with a refreshed outlook. *Whatever troubles you had yesterday...leave them there and start today with new energy.* Sometimes (*actually, most of the time*) we have a bad habit of carrying over our worries into a new, fresh day. **We weren't woken up this morning to sit around and dwell on yesterday**, our past, or our failures. Every new day is a fresh start to turn it all around.

Today's Daily Affirmation is:

I will embrace all that life throws my way because I can handle it.

Life has a lot of ups and downs. No one is exempt from going through them either – not the richest or the most famous. **The journey is teaching you lessons that you'll need at your destination.** So don't focus on the destination, pay close attention to your journey – that's where you'll acquire *wisdom*.

Today's Daily Affirmation is:

I trust myself and my intuition.

Those questions in your head or your heart are being answered for you – the Universe (God) is always speaking, you just have to be quiet long enough to hear him. **Patience and a listening ear will get you far in this world.** *You'll be shocked to discover that you will find what you need in the places you least expected it.*

Today's Daily Affirmation is:

I trust that everything will work out the way it was meant to.

We all know that one person who can handle situations with grace, ease, and peace. They could sit calmly if the house were burning down around them. Aren't we all striving for that kind of peace in our lives? Stop worrying and start realizing that whatever happens, is going to happen and sometimes things are out of our control. We just have to **_give it to God, leave it in the hands of the Universe, and trust it'll all be taken care of._**

Today's Daily Affirmation is:

I have so much more beauty left to experience in this life.

There are days that we feel stuck. Stuck in a situation, a mentality, a job, a relationship, a mood. We're all human, and we're going to have ups and downs. But what I want to remind you of today is that **_there's so much more ahead for you that you have yet to see and experience._** Realize that all those frustrations; all those tears **will be paid back to you tenfold very soon.** Life always...*ALWAYS* comes full circle.

Today's Daily Affirmation is:

I accept the challenge of learning all I can from those around me.

The Universe places people in your path throughout the course of your life for a reason – *not all of them are meant to stay in your life forever.* They might stick around for a second, a week, or even a few years. **Cherish what they are there to do.** Enjoy their company while you have it and learn what you need to learn from them. They are there to guide and teach you lessons, and sometimes their job is never done, and sometimes it wraps quicker than you'd expect.

Today's Daily Affirmation is:

Fear has no place in my life. I am at peace in all that I do.

Fear is a funny thing. If we stop allowing it to overcome us and take over our lives, it will no longer hinder us. Yes, I said **"Allow"** it. The *spirit of fear* is not given, but it haunts us, and we allow it to take over way too often.

Let it go – release the fear, stop worrying, and **allow peace to take over your body.** Once you are able to recognize and conquer *the need to control* – and just let things be how they're going to be, and unfold how they're meant to, you will rid your life of fear forever.

Today's Daily Affirmation is:

I will be authentic and loving to everyone who crosses my path today.

If you want to receive love in your life, you need to give love. I don't mean just show you care to the closest people around you either – I mean have a spirit of love in your heart. *Be giving, gracious, and humble.* Exude love in all realms of your life – from waiting in the line at Starbucks to picking up your kids at school. **The moment your aura and the energy you are giving out demonstrates a pure, genuine love – you'll be like a magnet for the same to return to you.**

Today's Daily Affirmation is:

When I release my need to worry, everything takes care of itself.

Rest, relax, and recharge. Align your energy with your attitude to match your positive spirit. Take today to release any worries, any stress you might be holding inside and let it go. Nothing is holding you back. Nothing is stopping you. Nothing can block you unless you allow it. Breathe and now exhale. You are pure divine love, and nothing and nobody can stand in your way!

Today's Daily Affirmation is:

I am open to all opportunities today.

Today is full of brand new opportunities. Today has never ever happened before. You never know where it could take you, and the anticipation and excitement should be brewing for you now as you read this. ***Take today to look at things differently.***

A quote I heard long ago is, *"If you keep doing what you're doing, you'll keep getting what you got."* So switch it up, take a different approach…breathe life into your heart, mind, and spirit knowing that all is well as long as you say it's well – you never know what could be until you choose to believe.

Today's Daily Affirmation is:

I will not allow my circumstances to define who I am on the inside.

You are not stuck in your circumstances. *You are not defined by what others think about you.* You are who you believe you are and just because things may not be where you want them to be right now – doesn't mean they won't end up there. Don't worry what others think of you, don't wait for reassurance or validation. Believe in **YOUR** soul and where it's desiring to go.

Today's Daily Affirmation is:

I'm excited for what's to come.

Get excited for what your immediate future holds! You're on this path, this journey for a reason and where it takes you, only you can decide. ***Have faith in yourself and the process and trust that God will always guide your steps.**

Today's Daily Affirmation is:

I will not allow outside forces to affect my internal peace.

Once you can better understand what's going on in the Universe – you'll be better prepared to handle anything thrown your way. If you know that no matter what it looks like...it's HELPING you...then nothing at all can ever sway you. With that said, *focus on you today and try not to let anxieties take over your body.* Sure, things might not go as planned – but **everything works out and comes full circle eventually.** So just stay in peace and trust that eventually you will see that beautiful masterpiece you desire within you.

Today's Daily Affirmation is:

I will breathe my way into a peaceful day.

Sometimes we start stressing out about things beyond our control, hindering our divine flow – yet not even realizing we're doing so until later. **Don't sweat the small stuff.** There are way more important things to think about other than how bad the traffic was on the drive to work or why the weather sucks outside. There is something larger working behind the scenes, but we often get hung up on our external conditions rather than our innate inner peace. Trust that even if something isn't going *YOUR* way, *it's still going the way it was meant to go.*

Today's Daily Affirmation is:

I will take one day at a time and focus on the good.

Focus on the present moment. Don't worry about what could have been or what should happen – *we need not worry about the future.* Because right NOW is creating the future. What you focus on in this very moment will be what shapes tomorrow and the next day and the next. Maintain your peace. Everything might not be going the right way around you, but you can't let it affect your energy. Keep your mind focused on what you desire to feel, think, and see and allow that to seep into your energy and co-create your reality..

Today's Daily Affirmation is:

I will let my truth speak for me and guide my steps. Fear no longer hinders my life.

Intuition is a wonderful and powerful tool that we all have within us. Some are more sensitive to it (*more intuitive*) while others tend to ignore it. **Never ignore that voice inside you** – it only speaks when you need to listen.

Sometimes people sweep it to the side because they know it's right, but they aren't ready to face the reality of what it's telling them. Others rely so heavily on their intuition that they're susceptible to letting negativity sneak in – thus confusing them. **Don't ever let the voice of Fear speak louder than the Truth** – especially in your spirit.

How do you tell the difference? As long as you're in a mindset of peace – then the **Truth** will speak up! Fear speaks when you're nervous, negative, anxious, angry, etc.

Today's Daily Affirmation is:

I will pursue my unique talents because that will bring me the ultimate happiness.

What's holding you back from pursuing your dream? Worry? Doubt? Fear? Finances? Confidence? If you have a passion or vision, chase it – don't deny yourself from living the life you were meant to live. We weren't put on this Earth to question our abilities or our existence. We weren't placed here *just* to do something for the money. **We were all put here for a purpose** – and we all have our own, individual, unique purposes. When you reach that turning point of realizing that you were meant to do something bigger than what you've been doing – don't find every excuse to ignore it. **Don't overthink your dreams.**

Today's Daily Affirmation is:

*I am not my own worst enemy.
If I believe I can, I will.*

We can be our own worst enemy. Maybe you are hard on yourself because you are not where you want to be in life. Or maybe someone else is discouraging you or placing doubts in your mind. *We are all intelligent creatures*, but we all learn in different ways.

Some people learn best in a traditional school setting – while others thrive in on-the-job experience environments. Some can learn simply by watching or listening, while others need to be shown and guided, step-by-step a few times over. No one is better than you, and I believe that no one is smarter than you.

You are as smart as you allow yourself to be. Walking through life curious, with an open mind will allow your brain to function better than someone who walks around flashing their fancy resume with their fancy schooling. Here's the thing – don't be discouraged and don't get down on yourself. *Stop comparing yourself, your experience, and your journey in life to others around you.* **You are what you say you are; you can do what you believe you can do.** Don't let anyone ever tell you what you can't do.

Today's Daily Affirmation is:

I am looking forward to what's to come.

Start your day with a positive, hopeful spirit – like you have something to look forward to, even though you might not. Remember, **what you think, you create** – so think positive and you attract positive energy. Think negative and you attract negativity.

Today's Daily Affirmation is:

I love who I am and celebrate all that I've accomplished.

Focus on your accomplishments today. Don't get down on yourself for things you might not have done yet. ***Celebrate yourself for all you have done thus far in your life.*** Give yourself the love and attention you deserve and remember that if you took a breath this morning, then there's still a lot for you to look forward to in life.

Today's Daily Affirmation is:

I wish good things for all people who cross my path, even those who don't wish me well. The Universe will take care of them in due time.

You're going to encounter a lot of people throughout your life. Some will love you, support you, and appreciate you. Others will envy you, reject you, and disrespect you. **You cannot let those who have nothing nice to say affect your mood, spirit, or dreams.**

Psychologically there are many reasons people will act in a negative manner, but without getting into all that, there is a very simple way to handle people who don't wish you well. **Wish them well.** Yes, you heard me correctly – don't curse those who curse you – bless those, who curse you. Everybody's favorite long lost cousin *"Karma"* always comes back around. What you reap is what you sow – so remember, walk in confidence and don't let anything or anyone break your spirit.

Today's Daily Affirmation is:

Personal growth is important to me. I am aware of my thoughts and feelings in all circumstances.

Self-awareness is something that not a lot of people have, but it's something that's required for individual growth. We all have that friend that always likes to be surrounded by people. They don't like having any downtime; they never enjoy being alone. **If you can sit alone, listening to your inner most thoughts and enjoy it – that's the first crucial step into being self-aware.** Practice this today, even if just for a couple of minutes and take note of how much you learn about yourself in those few minutes of solitude.

Today's Daily Affirmation is:

I choose to stay true to myself always by appreciating and respecting the person I've become.

Celebrate yourself! Take today to focus on how much you've grown and what you've accomplished. Every day should be focused on love, so give yourself the love you deserve. **Treat yourself** – take yourself out to eat, pamper yourself at the spa or splurge on a chocolatey dessert just for you. You can celebrate love without having a significant other. **The most important lesson to note is you won't find true love until you can truly love yourself.** Do some soul searching and learn how to appreciate, respect, and love who **YOU** are.

Today's Daily Affirmation is:

My actions, thoughts, and words towards others impact my own life. I will only put out what I want to receive.

Have you ever asked yourself what is your purpose in life? It's quite a loaded question, isn't it? Though we all have different dreams, goals, and passions – we all have a very similar **"purpose"** here on Earth. *Do right by others and help those in need because what we put out, we get back.* It's all a very basic method: Think positive, attract positivity. Think happy, attract happiness. Think negative, attract negativity.

We are like magnets – all of us are, no matter your belief system, you are still susceptible to the Universal energy that what goes around, comes around. So if you're hoping for **"good"** things to happen in your life, do good for others. It doesn't matter how small or big the **"good deed"** is. It's the *authentic and honest energy that you exert* that will bring the goodness into your life.

Today's Daily Affirmation is:

My potential is limitless.

You are full of potential. Maybe you've been in the same position for a while, but that doesn't mean you're stuck there forever. ***Circumstances can change in a split second.*** Opportunities can arise when you least expect them. Change is something that consistently happens. Just because it hasn't crossed your path yet, doesn't mean it won't.

Today's Daily Affirmation is:

I am capable and well-equipped to handle any situation that comes my way.

If you're human, then you're going to experience emotions, and not always the good kind. We are going to get discouraged, hurt, angry, confused, upset, and sometimes depressed. It comes with the territory of being alive. You can't avoid or hide from them. But you can learn how to deal with them. **You can better equip yourself to handle any situation thrown at you if you can learn to control your thoughts.** If you can filter and process the information that comes your way with the basic mindset that *everything happens for a reason,* and *it is what it is*, you can ride that roller coaster of emotions more smoothly than ever before.

Today's Daily Affirmation is:

I accept that everything happens for a reason.

I often get a lot of people coming to me saying how they feel stuck – in bad financial situations, relationships, jobs or just life circumstances. They feel like they've been **"stuck"** for quite some time – like they can't seem to catch a break and don't understand why things haven't changed for the better.

Sometimes we're kept in a situation, whether we like it or not, because we're meant to learn something there. Sometimes it doesn't matter how good of a person we are, how giving we are, how nice we are or even how hard we work at something – *God is going to keep us in that situation for a reason until we learn the lesson we need to learn.*

You see sometimes it takes *drastic measures* to teach us, *stubborn humans,* a lesson. And more times than not, it takes extreme circumstances to make us change our thinking, behavior, and ways. You need to trust the process though and understand that no matter the situation, **something better is waiting on the other side**.

Today's Daily Affirmation is:

I will live every moment and learn from it.

Our circumstances do not dictate our future. *Our current situation does not describe who we are* – it's merely what we're dealing with. Do you believe that life is not about the destination, but rather about the journey itself? It might sound cliché, but it is the truth.

So maybe you're unemployed…that doesn't describe your character as a human being. That doesn't mean you're not a good person with a kind soul. You just haven't encountered the job for you yet. Maybe you are not in the financial state that you hoped you would be in at your age. That doesn't mean that it can't change at any second.

We are all put in situations for a reason. Maybe it's part of our journey to help someone else learn a lesson as they observe what we go through. Maybe it has to teach us something important – like to be grateful for what we do have, instead of wishing we had something different. Whatever it is – whatever you're going through right now, at this very moment, stop and think…**how is this helping me? What is this teaching me? Is someone else learning something from me?** I promise you that you will have an answer for at least one of those questions if not all three and then some. **Focus and enjoy each moment in your life, every situation that is thrown your way because there is value there.** Isn't that what life's all about? Learning to be the best *"you"* that you can be?!

Today's Daily Affirmation is:

I will not accept defeat.

Feeling defeated? It's normal. Your energy's low and things aren't going as they should. Don't sink into the pit of despair just yet, because **"change"** is a powerful thing that happens when you least expect it and when you need it most. ***Your circumstances can turn around, a new opportunity could arise, and a door could open just for you.*** But if your eyes are closed and you've shut out the world, you'll never see the good in what's coming right around the corner.

Today's Daily Affirmation is:

I will be patient. Everything that is meant to be, will be, in due time.

Timing is everything. I know you have heard that before and unfortunately, yet fortunately, it's very true. Sometimes the things we *"want"* don't happen when we *"want"* them to because the timing isn't right. God has a bigger plan for us, and though we have free will, divine intervention is a funny thing. Beyond our control things can stop and go, and all we can do is be patient and have faith that **when the time is right, the right thing will take place**.

Today's Daily Affirmation is:

I recognize that I need to focus on what will only help me grow as a human being. I will not sweat the small stuff.

Silence your mind. Do you hear that voice in your head; that impending intuition that is speaking to you. You need to listen to it; it will not steer you wrong. Meditation is a wonderful tool to ground yourself, clear your thoughts, and focus on your path. It helps to open your mind's eye to what you need to be focusing on.

I like to call it **"clearing the clutter"** out of your brain. You know that saying *"don't sweat the small stuff"*? In a sense, that is what meditation will help you achieve – focusing on what you should be doing to grow, achieve, and reach your highest potential, no matter what your life's path is.

Today's Daily Affirmation is:

I am as wise as I allow myself to be

True wisdom and insight are free because we all have them it inside of us. Some of us are just more in tune to it than others. **Learn to tap into your inner wisdom** – it is a powerful tool that can advance you far beyond what you would expect. Once you open it up, you won't be able to shut it off.

Today's Daily Affirmation is:

I am capable of so much more than I give myself credit for. I am equipped to handle any situation because I am strong.

Stop searching for that person who's going to **'save'** you or change your life. They don't exist. I know, it's harsh, but the reality is this – look in your mirror. *You see that person staring back at you?* **That's the only person that's going to 'save' you.**

Everything you need is already inside you. *God does not send us out into this world ill-equipped.* It's not possible to live a life that is "perfect" but it is possible to live an imperfect life, perfectly. If we're honest with ourselves, then we realize that we wouldn't know how to appreciate all the good stuff without **"pain"**. **Pain will teach you how to pray.** *If there is no struggle, there is no progress.* Here's a great example my Pastor gave in church that makes understanding this concept **SO** much easier: The idea of going to a gym is to get stronger. To get stronger, you have to lift weights – you have to lift something heavy. You can't go to a gym and lift paper and expect to get stronger. If you can lift the *'heavy'* stuff in the gym and in *'life'* you **WILL** get stronger, and it'll get easier to lift the heavy stuff later.

Today's Daily Affirmation is:

I refuse to feed into the negativity

Are you struggling with something? Experiencing turmoil in a certain part of your life? Take a step back and look at yourself and your situation honestly. **Now is a time for reflection**, and maybe your situation seems a lot worse because you've let it affect your **attitude.** We're all human, so it happens, but you need to muster up a little bit of strength and realize that everything happens for a reason – good things, bad things, all things **HAPPEN** for a **REASON**.

Once you recognize that and **accept it,** look at your attitude. *Yes, right now –* take a good hard look at it. *Are you negative about your situation?* It might be easy to be. You might even have every excuse in the book to be negative about your situation. But ***negativity*** is a funny, sneaky little thing. It seeps into your brain without you realizing it and acts as a bouncy ball, bouncing from one situation to the next – or even one person to the next.

So you need to stop it dead in its tracks. *Check yourself, check your attitude,* ***be grateful*** because things could **ALWAYS** be a lot worse and realize that attitude is everything. You could change your situation around in a heartbeat if you just start looking at it differently.

Today's Daily Affirmation is:

I have a purpose in this life and I will treasure it, enjoy it, and embrace it

You have a purpose. It could be small or big – it doesn't matter the size though because we are each placed on this Earth for a purpose. To change, learn, impact, teach, love, enjoy, and the list goes on and on.

Do you know what your purpose is? It's okay not to know. The best way to find out is to silence your mind, pay attention, and listen to your world – the world around you. *Do people keep coming to you for advice?* Maybe you're everybody's motivator or work-out partner. Perhaps your house is the go-to place for dinner parties because you are an amazing cook.

Look, some of this might sound menial to you, but *you're making an impact* whether you're keeping people in shape, providing relationship advice or simply cooking dinner. I want you to understand that even if you're just babysitting some kids or keeping your grandmother company in the afternoon, you still have a purpose and it's very important. You are teaching someone something, you are keeping someone company that would otherwise be lonely, and *you're probably learning just as much from them as they are from you.*

Today's Daily Affirmation is:

I have faith that my blessing is right around the corner

Your miracle is near; your blessing is right around the corner. Don't doubt it, have faith. So what if things are bad – they'll get better. **You can't be stuck in the valley forever – eventually, you'll be climbing to the top of the mountain.**

Life is never going to have you travel one flat surface – hills, valleys, twists, and turns are just part of everyone's journey. ***You are not alone***; without struggle you can't experience joy, without sadness, we wouldn't know happiness.

Today's Daily Affirmation is:

I acknowledge that change starts within me. I choose happiness and love.

What if you could wake up every morning and acknowledge all the great things you did yesterday? What if you could stop being so hard on yourself? What if you allowed love to permeate every ounce of your body?

Having a better perspective on your life is where change begins. It starts within you. If you can look at things differently and appreciate things more, rather than negating everything, you will begin to see that life is pretty beautiful and not as bad as you're making it out to be. **It all starts with you.** Make up your mind right now that you will no longer be so hard on yourself; that you will allow love to fill your soul, and that will stop you from taking what you have for granted.

Today's Daily Affirmation is:

I acknowledge that the Universe will locate my missing pieces and help me to learn, grow stronger, and become a better person if I just trust in its process.

We all need to go through things to get places. ***Sometimes we're meant to be broken to have the right pieces placed back together.*** Like a jigsaw puzzle, perhaps the only way that missing piece can be found or made to fit is if we take the entire puzzle apart. Or maybe it just needs to sit, as it is, in its *unfinished form until the time is right* for the missing piece to be found.

Today's Daily Affirmation is:

I acknowledge that there's a lesson in every battle. If there was no struggle, there would be no progress.

We are all going through something – battling something internally daily. It could be disease or sickness. It could be depression and anxiety. It could be financial problems or worries about your children or your job. None of us live perfect lives, though we are all striving to live the best life we can live.

I want you to really listen to what I'm about to say – focus on it and keep it in your memory: **this slight affliction is just for a moment.** This suffering, this struggle that you're going through, is only for a brief moment in time. My pastor has said that sometimes people wonder, *"How do people stay faithful to a cause when the cause doesn't seem faithful to them?"* How do you stay faithful to your God or your beliefs when you're going through something? *You remember, it's only for a moment and that the same God who brought you through it last time, will bring you through it again.*

Today's Daily Affirmation is:

I accept change into my life and acknowledge all the seeds I've worked so hard to sow, are about to bloom.

Were you starting to lose hope? **Don't – change is coming and not the bad kind either!**

Today's Daily Affirmation is:

I'm on the verge of a breakthrough and I will not let the Devil get the best of me now.

The saying goes that things always get worse before they get better. You ever notice you are about to break, snap, and go off right before a breakthrough happens? It happens to all of us, including myself.

When you reach that pinnacle point, I want you to recognize it and take a deep breath. **The Devil works his hardest when you're about to win and that's why he tries really hard to make you lose your mind right before something great is about to happen.** Don't let him win – this is when you really need to keep your mind right, stay focused on the prize, and breathe in the positive energy. Start confessing you've already won and before you know it your breakthrough will be here!

Today's Daily Affirmation is:

I stand firm in my beliefs that everything will turn out okay in the end.

It's negativity's job to make you lose hope. Included in its job description is making you feel like you are lying to yourself when you feel like something good will happen. You are not lying to yourself. *That feeling of hope you have sitting in your gut, it's telling you the truth.* But negativity is strong, and if you let it, it'll easily wipe out that last bit of hope you have left. Don't let it win. Stand firm in your belief that everything will turn around because let me tell you something: **everything is always okay in the end, if it's not okay, then it's not the end.**

Today's Daily Affirmation is:

I am unique and talented. I promise to share my special gifts with the world.

Stop caring what others say about you. Stop caring what they think of you. Stop comparing yourself to them or their journey in life. *There is only one of you, and you need to strive to be the best you that you can be.* Focus on your talents and remember how unique and beautiful you are; inside and out.

Once you stop focusing on outside factors and start focusing on your internal ones, you'll realize just how talented and special you are.

Today's Daily Affirmation is:

I am determined to have a positive impact on as many lives as I can.

You were put here for a purpose. Everyone has a purpose. You might not have discovered yours yet, and that is ok. Maybe your purpose isn't meant to take effect until later in life. Maybe you discovered yours early – or maybe, just maybe you have more than one. Whichever it may be, believe in yourself and don't give up. *If life seems too hard right now – it always gets really bad before it gets really good. I promise you that.*

Today's Daily Affirmation is:

I will not be swayed by excessive emotions. I will be still and wait for the truth.

Staying grounded isn't always an easy thing to do. We as humans have so much going on around us that provoke emotions and thoughts, that it's easy to lose our way and sometimes lose our mind. Some people don't fully understand what being grounded means – essentially it means being **"well balanced and sensible."** Not letting external forces provoke your internal feelings.

Some people just have a nature about them; it's in their personality, and they can keep others grounded – while others turn to meditation, prayer, and even The Bible to keep their feet planted firmly on the ground. **Whatever your method is, embrace it.** The important thing is to recognize that you are human, and you are going to experience emotions; fear, sadness, happiness, anxiety, joy, kindness, etc.

The key to being grounded is not allowing those emotions to get the best of you. Not allowing them to overlap or cover up what you truly feel about a person or situation. Sometimes the best way to do that is to silence yourself, breathe in, breathe out, and let the emotion run over you like a wave. Once it passes, and you let it go, you will begin to see the truth expose itself.

Today's Daily Affirmation is:

I promise to appreciate all the wonderful things I already have in my life

Sometimes we're so busy looking at what's ahead of us, that we miss what's standing right in front of us. Don't get too busy that you miss life as it's happening in front of you. **Don't get so caught up in the future that you miss the present.** Sometimes we are focusing on the things we want, wish we had, and hope to get, that we take for granted all the beautiful things we already have in our lives.

Today's Daily Affirmation is:

I will live in the now and allow miracles to work their magic for me.

You know that John Lennon quote, *"Life is what happens when you are busy making other plans"*? Don't let that hold true for your life. I like to say, **"Miracles are what happen when you're busy making other plans."** Essentially you should be focusing on your life and enjoy every second of it – but it's while you're doing that, that those things that you least expect to happen, happen.

Those things that you used to be dwelling on, hoping and wishing for seem to sneak right into our lives when we're occupied with paying attention to things happening in the 'now.' **So focus on the 'now' and let everything else work it's magic while you do that** – because it will, I promise.

Today's Daily Affirmation is:

I choose above all else, happiness.

Are you surrounded by people who are constantly dragging you down? Questioning your abilities? Trying too hard to influence you to go in a direction you don't want to go in? If the answer is yes, then you need to make a decision right now on who you're living your life for. Is it for them? If it is then you have no reason to complain. But if you're choosing to live your life for yourself…to make yourself happy then you need to take a step back and **remind yourself that words have no power over you unless you let them.** No one can dictate your life unless you let them. No one can influence your decisions unless you allow them to. Never, ever live your life for someone else. **It's ok to share your life with others, but first, you need to make yourself happy.**

Today's Daily Affirmation is:

I choose to look past the hate and continue to give and receive love.

You are going to encounter people in your life who have too much pride to admit when they're wrong; who are too stubborn to change. Who simply do not want to give you the credit you deserve for the wisdom you have or the things you accomplish in life. They take but do not give. They discredit and discourage you. They attack and criticize and are not receptive to any advice in return (*some call these "haters"*).

Sometimes these people are going to flock to you because positive energy is magnetic and it'll attract all sorts of things (*you'd be surprised!*). Don't let it deter you from the path you're on. Don't let it discourage you, worry, frustrate or even anger you. Even if you are unable to get through to them, they are flocking to you because they want to feed on your energy and wisdom. Look at it as a compliment – even if they don't want your advice their subconscious does. **Look past their faults and realize that their soul is in need of a little bit of what you have.** That's what's important – not the angry human on the outside, the soul on the inside.

Today's Daily Affirmation is:

I am thankful for what I have and I am excited for what's to come.

Stop looking at the things you don't have, and start looking at the things you do have. **The things you are taking for granted, someone else is praying for.** Don't lose yourself so much in your hopes and dreams that you lose sight of everything you already have going for you. Remember to thank God for the blessings he has already given you and trust that he will take care of you by bringing you the things you need, exactly when you need them.

Today's Daily Affirmation is:

I will stop fighting my circumstances and trust the Universe to deliver on time.

What do you do when life exhausts you? I hope **'give up'** isn't your answer. Circumstances aren't always going to go the way we want them to, but most of the time that's because there's a better way for them to go.

Rejection is protection, and it's true what they say – that when one door closes, another one opens, perhaps even a window as well. Universal timing is everything, and so I hope if you're getting exhausted with your situation, **you realize that if the timing isn't right for it to take place now – the right time will soon come.**

Today's Daily Affirmation is:

I will always remember to keep an open mind, open heart, and never limit my vision.

I read an article that said that whenever we perceive a lack of something (*be it money, food, time, etc.*), we become so absorbed by it that our thinking becomes altered. It went on to say that **"scarcity captures the mind."**

For instance, if you're driving in a snowstorm, your focus is on the road ahead of you due to the dangerous conditions. You are limited from observing things you might have noticed on a sunny day. That means road signs, billboards, trees, anything in your periphery. You've limited your thinking and your perception because, in this case, safety was your focus. The saying goes, **"Don't lose sight of the forest for the trees."** Don't be so focused on one beautiful tree that you forget about all the other millions of trees in the forest. Don't become so involved in the little details that you lose sight of the big picture.

Today's Daily Affirmation is:

I promise to forgive myself, it's the only way I'm going to make any progress in life.

Forgiveness is a word a lot of us don't like to hear and yet it's crucial to forgive not only others but also yourself. *Have you been holding a grudge against yourself?* You're not alone – we all do it at some point in time. Here's the thing, if you have or if you are, tell yourself you're sorry. **It's time to move on now. It's time to let it go and let it be in the past.** You can't move forward if you're constantly staring in the rear-view mirror. You need to start looking through the windshield and let go of what's behind you – and that all starts with forgiveness.

Today's Daily Affirmation is:

I love myself enough to surround myself with love.

Are you surrounding yourself with people that are bringing you down? Separate yourself from them. If your crowd isn't building you up, you need to find a new one. ***If you crowd isn't showing you how to tweak and better yourself, find a new one.*** Don't surround yourself with people who only praise you – **surround yourself with people who teach you, love you and mutually respect you.**

Today's Daily Affirmation is:

I am at peace knowing the darkness has lifted. I acknowledge the Universe is working in my favor.

We go through seasons of rebirth and renewal where **everything you have been manifesting starts to take bloom.** Be patient and watch it unfold. All heaviness will lift off your spirit, and doubt will clear your mind as you begin to reap your rewards and watch the seeds you've sewn take root and blossom.

Maybe you just learned a hard lesson that the Universe has been trying to teach you, or perhaps all those prayers you've been praying are starting to take effect. No matter what you've been going through know that when the rain stops, the sun always comes out. But for the flowers to grow, the ground must get a little wet!

Today's Daily Affirmation is:

I am brave and unique. I will always exude authenticity.

Staying true to who you are requires bravery. It takes guts to be 100% authentic all the time. But it's what you need to do. Your personality shouldn't shift around different groups of friends, and keep in mind that there's a huge difference between being polite and being fake. **Remember that when you are being the real you, all the time, you will attract the right people and situations into your life.** Your energy is magnetic, so don't mask it behind a persona.

Today's Daily Affirmation is:

I am thankful for all that I have.

Take today to do something nice for yourself, or for someone else. It doesn't matter if it's a stranger or someone close to you. It could even be for your dog/cat. Release your anger, frustration and fear today. **Cast it out of your mind, body and soul and focus on the good that is about to take place in your life.** Cherish what you have, because there is so much more coming your way.

Today's Daily Affirmation is:

I will stay positive no matter what. Negativity will not consume me.

Stop feeling sorry for yourself. You don't attract anything positive putting out that energy, all you do is negate what good things are meant to happen. You also push away everything you've been striving to become.

Consider this – **a negative + a negative always = negative.** A negative + a positive = a negative **IF** the positive number is **less** than the negative number. (i.e.: - 4 + 3 = -1 **BUT** - 4 + 5 = 1) *So what exactly does this mean and how does this apply to your life?*

Simple – **your positives need to outweigh your negatives.** All the time – no buts about it. You need to fight through the negative, stop feeling sorry for yourself and keep affirming all these wonderfully positive things about you and your life. **Eventually, those negative thoughts will fade so far into the distance you'll forget they were once front and center in your life.**

Today's Daily Affirmation is:

I accept I cannot control everything.

Take a break. It's allowed, and you totally deserve it! Listen to your body, mind, and soul. Meditate, take a nap or catch up on your reading. **Whatever you're going through can, and WILL, work itself out – don't waste your last bit of energy worrying over it.** Allow the Universe to do its job while you take a 24-hour break. I bet everything will look clearer the minute you step away from it and relax a little in your brain. God is always working...so you don't need to. Sometimes when we try to control it all mentally, we simply get in the way. Step away and breathe...let God do his thing!

Today's Daily Affirmation is:

I am sure of who I am. The opinions of others do not hurt me.

It's not possible to live a life that's perfect. But if we're honest with ourselves we'll live a life that is perfect for us. That means you need to stop caring how others perceive you. Stop caring who is gossiping about you or hating on you. That is their problem, not yours. Their opinion of you is just that, their opinion. Now – *don't get it twisted* – you can **"not care"** about other opinions, but that doesn't mean you ignore your words or actions. That also doesn't mean you don't continually try to better yourself in all aspects of your life. If you're self-aware of who you are and what you're doing, that is all that matters.

Today's Daily Affirmation is:

I will let it go.

There will come a point in your life when you'll realize why you were meant to let some things go. It is then when everything will slowly begin to make sense. **Our paths are the way they are for a reason – we are meant to encounter certain individuals and deal with particular circumstances – all for the benefit of our growth.**

A lot of times people don't want to let things go, whether it's people, arguments, or just situations in general. Understand that if it's leaving you or it's time for you to leave it, do it with grace, dignity and understanding that it's for a good reason. **The things that are meant to be a part of your life forever will return in due time.**

Today's Daily Affirmation is:

I have faith that whatever happens is in my best interest.

When things don't go your way, don't freak out. They are not always going to happen when we want them to happen. Most of the time, they definitely will not happen when we want them to happen.

You know how I've said that your thoughts create your reality? What you think at any time of the day will manifest situations and their outcomes. That doesn't necessarily mean that if you think something won't happen, it's just not going to happen – but if you're worried about it **NOT** happening, all that energy you're putting out there negating it will slow down the process of it happening.

So today if you find yourself dwelling or obsessing about something, anything – stop yourself dead in your tracks. Now focus your attention on telling yourself that ***'you know God heard you, and the Universe is working in your favor, and you trust that whatever the outcome will be, it will be what you need in your life right now.'***

Today's Daily Affirmation is:

I will treat others how I want to be treated.

Empathy is an important trait to have. The capacity to recognize emotions that are being experienced by another person, animal, etc. I've often heard from people that they feel like they're getting a dose of their own medicine; **like certain behaviors they used to have, but have since outgrown have now chased them down through other people.**

The Universe will do this to you – to **TEACH** you a lesson. *Do we ever really know how we made someone else feel until we're made to feel the same way?* Especially if that feeling was not so pleasant? We don't really know how it felt when we broke so-and-so's heart until someone comes along and breaks our heart in the same way.

If you're experiencing a *'dose of your own medicine'* lately, don't worry, just acknowledge that there's a lesson there for you. Be empathetic towards that other individual because you were probably in that person's shoes at some point in your lifetime. Until you place yourself **BACK** into that position and recognize **HOW** you were feeling then, you'll never pass the test.

Today's Daily Affirmation is:

I am listening and receiving the Universal signs.

It's amazing the places I get messages from – sometimes out of thin air, music, or while I'm sleeping. Other times during meditation, a cup of tea, while watching TV, or while browsing online and **BAM** something straight-up hits me in the face (*no, not literally – that'd be weird*).

One time I signed online, was doing some blogging and social media work, and I get this message, **"A time of positive change. A situation suddenly moves forward. Fortune is on your side."** Then I pour myself a cup of tea and the teabag read: **"When we practice listening, we become intuitive."** A few hours later I decide upon another cup of tea, same flavor – I open the tea bag, to my surprise it says, *"When we practice listening, we become intuitive"* OK, ok… I get it; I hear you LOUD and clear! Just to be clear, this never happens – or at least has never happened to me. Sure there's 'x' amount of teabags in a box, and for as long as I've been drinking this tea and I've never had a repeat message – let alone in the same day, hours apart.

I'm sure you're thinking *'what's the big deal?'* or better yet, *'Amy, where's my affirmation?'* I'm getting there right now! **When you STOP looking, you'll find what you're seeking**. When I'm searching for a sign or a message, I can't seem to get one even when I start praying and begging for one. But when I stop focusing on it, the Universe delivers it to me – sometimes on my TV screen, sometimes in my tea cup. So earlier I said that *'a situation suddenly moves forward',* and so I want to leave you with this – **whatever you're dealing with, you will get through**. Be still and practice **LISTENING** to everything around you – the signs are there, and they are being delivered to help you remain patient and tell you what to do next. Don't **LOOK** for them…**LISTEN**.

Today's Daily Affirmation is:

I will remain grounded because my breakthrough is here.

Something new is on the horizon. You are on the verge of healing, of accomplishing something you have been working really hard at – you're on the verge of *FINALLY (yes, finally)* seeing that breakthrough. Stay grateful, humble, faithful and happy. Everything is working in your favor – you have to believe it before you can see it.

Today's Daily Affirmation is:

I recognize that no response, is a response.

Have you ever prayed or meditated and gotten no response? Nothing, zip, zilch, nada – just silence?! **Sometimes no response is a response.** They say silence is deadly – but silence from God or the Angels or the Universe is simply, *"you're right where you should be."*

Don't get frustrated when you don't get an answer. Don't get mad at God/Universe/Angels if they give you the good old-fashioned silent treatment. Understand that it's just their way of saying they are busy working on *'it'* and you're doing everything right. You're heading in the right direction and when the time is right and they need to deliver you a message or some directions on where to head next – trust me they'll get your attention. So enjoy the silence – revel in it because it's a good sign, a reassuring one - and say *"Thank You"* as you acknowledge their hard work in your life too.

Today's Daily Affirmation is:

I deserve everything I wish for. I promise to stop being my own worst enemy.

You are worthy of everything you want. You deserve it – stop telling yourself that you don't. **Stop being your own worst enemy.** You are only delaying all those promises from coming to light. You are delaying the inevitable positive outcome with your negative thoughts against yourself. **STOP!**

Today's Daily Affirmation is:

I will lift the heaviness off my heart and forgive myself finally.

How do you expect to move forward in life if you cannot forgive yourself? Forgiving yourself first is more important than forgiving others (*no, I'm not saying you shouldn't forgive others*) – but I **AM** saying that before you can even do that, you need to forgive yourself **FIRST** and foremost.

If you can't forgive, it leads to anger, bitterness, frustration and depression. It also blocks your energy. *You know what that means?* All those good things you keep hoping, wishing and praying for cannot come to light and exist until you unblock your energy. That requires **forgiving** yourself for your past. **Forgiving** yourself for your mistakes. **Forgiving** for those choices you made that for some reason are making you feel sad or worse...guilty. **Forgiving** yourself for anything and everything so that you can finally leave it where it belongs – *in the past*...and move forward without the baggage.

Today's Daily Affirmation is:

I will exude empathy in all my encounters.

You cannot always change the things that happen to you or the way people treat you, but you can change the way you react to them. See half the battle is recognizing the situation for what it is, taking a deep breath and reacting (*no matter what*) with empathy, love and understanding.

You see there's always a reason for why people do/act the way they do. Always. You don't need to figure it out, but you do need to recognize that because that is what's going to give you the empathy. You never know what someone else is dealing with or going through unless you walk in their shoes – and the same goes the other way around. **So instead of worrying about how they're going to treat you, worry about how you're going to treat them.**

Today's Daily Affirmation is:

I will be authentic and live my truth.

Live your truth. Be authentic. Follow your passion. The biggest problem today is that people are so busy trying to change who they are and what they stand for depending on who they're around. **Stay true to who you are no matter where you are.** It's the only path to real, raw happiness.

Today's Daily Affirmation is:

I believe in me.

Do you believe *in yourself?* In *someone else?* In *something bigger?* It doesn't matter what you believe in, as long as you believe in something and the most important something is **YOU**. If you don't think you can do it, how do you expect others to believe you can do it? If you don't have faith in your decisions or your chosen path – how do you expect to get anywhere? Sure, it's a lot of questions – but they're valid ones.

Are you short-changing your potential? Do you doubt yourself? Stop doing that. Let go of the fear and worry. **Release the negative thoughts that enter your mind, telling you that you are incapable of something.** You are capable of anything and everything you put your mind to – *because what you put your mind on, the intentions you set – you give life to them.* So make sure you are giving life to good ones.

Today's Daily Affirmation is:

I am strong enough to realize that I can move on without some things holding me back.

Letting go doesn't mean you lost. Letting go doesn't mean you've given up. Some of us feel holding on makes us stronger. But, **_sometimes letting go means you're strong enough to realize that something better is waiting for you once you release your grip on what's holding you back._**

Today's Daily Affirmation is:

I will enjoy my life's journey and stop dwelling on the destination.

There are no accidents. Where you are right now in your life, on your journey is exactly where you are supposed to be. Do not question it anymore. Enjoy it. Learn from it. Take it all in. You will get to where you need to be in due time, but until then you are meant to learn things to prepare you for when you get there. So start enjoying the ride instead of stressing over the destination.

Today's Daily Affirmation is:

I claim my victory.

You've come a long way. **Where you've been is not where you are, and where you are is not where you'll stay.** You are constantly growing and improving – there is so much more waiting for you if you can just set yourself free of the restraints of your past and claim your victory!

Today's Daily Affirmation is:

I will always be mindful of my words and actions.

Words can hurt. Actions can also hurt – sometimes one hurts more than the other. Here's the thing, though – as long as you know your truth; who you are and what you stand for – it shouldn't matter what others say – but even then you will still get hurt at times. People are going to get mad. You'll even get mad sometimes and say things that hurt other people. Today I want you to be more mindful.

Be mindful of what you say and how you say it. *Because you never know what another person's going through and how your words will make them feel.* I watched this video called the Transformative Power of Music and a quote from it relates completely to today's affirmation. It was, **"I made a vow that I would never say anything that couldn't stand as the last thing I would say."**

Today's Daily Affirmation is:

I receive clarity and peace into my life.

Clarity is a beautiful thing. When you discover it it'll deliver you such peace in your life. Obtaining clarity isn't as challenging as you'd expect – prayer, meditation and being still can all help bring it to light. Regardless of your background or beliefs, sitting still in silence and being mindful of your thoughts can bring about a lot of answers. Today focus on receiving clarity from the Universe. Accept whatever information, advice and answers the Universe delivers to you – it all has its purpose and place in your life. **Receive it with grace and gratitude, because once your mind is clear, you can do amazing things.**

Today's Daily Affirmation is:

I will face my fears with confidence and I will win.

Dissolve your fears of failure and/or getting hurt. **They are only holding you back from your true potential and your soul's purpose in life.** Mentally you are going to have to battle the negative thoughts but they will eventually lose their power over you if you can learn to drown them out. You will finally be able to develop a method of casting them out the minute they sneak in and before you know it, they will feel as if they don't even exist at all. **Don't let the voices of fear and failure keep you from your dreams, visions, passions and goals.** Don't allow them the satisfaction of holding you back. Prove them wrong, you are worth so much more than they tell you that you are.

Today's Daily Affirmation is:

I am a walking miracle.

Believe it or not, you are a living miracle. **You are living evidence there is much more to this Universe than meets the eye.** Every time you have a breakthrough in your life, that is proof there's a God on your side. **You may not be where you want to be, but you need to be thankful you're not where you used to be.** Wherever God has planted you is exactly where you need to be right now. You need to be exactly where you are – so don't stress, don't dwell and don't try to figure it all out just take root and be at peace. God has brought you a long way – you are a walking miracle – living evidence, and if he's done it before, he'll do it again!

Today's Daily Affirmation is:

I acknowledge that my energy is magnetic and I will only attract what I exude.

Are you attracting the right people into your life? I'm not just talking about love interests – I mean in all aspects of your life – *are you attracting like-minded individuals?* **People who appreciate you and support you. People who can learn from you but also have something to teach you?**

The energy that you put out determines what you attract. So if you are drawing in the wrong types of people it is time to take a step back and look at yourself. What type of energy are you projecting? – and by that I don't mean just how personable or social you are – this also includes the energy that you savor internally. The energy you put into your thoughts. That silent, unspoken energy. Yes...even **THAT** is energy. Sure, people don't *'always'* know what you're thinking in that mind of yours, but let me tell you something – **the energy you put into your thoughts is still energy.** All energy is connected as one, just like we are all connected. Ever heard the saying *"6 degrees of separation"*? We won't get into that right now – but the point is that if you're thinking negative, you're going to attract negativity. If you're doubting yourself or your actions, things aren't exactly going to pan out in a positive way. If you exude confidence and think positively, you will attract just that.

Today's Daily Affirmation is:

I will remain at peace in all situations knowing that what is meant to be, will be no matter what I think.

Relax…there's no reason to stress, about anything. Don't freak out about things that are beyond your control. **The spirit of peace is what allows us to make rational decisions, not panic or fear or stress.** Let me tell you what happens when you freak out about something…anything. You allow your brain to get weak for that 1 split second of panic and you've opened the door for negativity to sneak in. Once it's in, it's not going to go quietly – you're going to have to drag it out, kicking and screaming. The only way to keep it out for good is to not unlock that deadbolt for it. That deadbolt needs to represent your rock solid peace in understanding that whatever is meant to be will be – **God will not give what belongs to you, to someone else.** So stop stressing, in due time everything will come together.

Today's Daily Affirmation is:

I appreciate my life.

When you look at other people's lives and wish you had what they have, you miss out on what you have going for yourself. We were each created uniquely different and yet we're all connected somehow, someway. But just because there's a Universal connection doesn't mean you need to lust after other people's blessings. For all you know, they could be wishing they had something you have. So here's the deal – **cherish yourself** – your life, personality, family, friends, blessings and curses. They are all yours. No one else can claim them or have them. They belong to you.

Today's Daily Affirmation is:

I recognize there is a lesson in every connection in life.

Ground yourself – keep your feet pressed firmly on the ground and remind yourself to stay humble. God has blessed you with all that you have – everything! **You wouldn't have been woken up this morning and reading this if you weren't blessed.** You wouldn't be able to breathe and function, work, love, joke, laugh, cry or even get angry without his blessings. *What you have can be taken away in a minute – then what will you be left with?* Material items are just that – material...they can come and go. That car of yours – you could turn around in 3 months and go trade it in. You could crash it and get a brand new one. Or it could simply break down on a long commute.

Devote your time to developing connections with things that won't come and go – non-material items. **These are the relationships that will stay for a lifetime – even if the humans themselves are no longer around.** Sure you can have a boyfriend/girlfriend and go "trade" them in for a new one a few months down the road – but what their soul gave you during your time together will be priceless (good **OR** bad). These are the relationships that will teach you the lessons you need to learn; provide you with the advice you're desperately seeking at that time for your life's journey. Give you the love you need and even the tears to cry. But there are lessons in all of this and these lessons allow your soul to grow. Recognizing this will keep you humble. So today remind yourself that there's a lesson in every connection!

Today's Daily Affirmation is:

I respect myself enough to chase down my dreams.

Charles Caleb Colton once said, "Imitation is the sincerest form of flattery." I beg to differ. Personally, I find imitation to be unoriginal. Here's the thing – each of us are uniquely different. I know I've written this before, but here we are again, and I remind you that we are each born with a purpose, and we each have our own individual hopes and dreams. *Why not embrace them?* – instead of seeing someone else doing something inspiring and trying to do the same thing. (this will result in you constantly seeking some form of happiness that you won't find until you embrace what's truly inside **YOU**.)

Now sure, there's obviously more than one person in the world dreaming of being an actor or a stock broker or some big wig executive somewhere, but what I want to reinforce today is to follow **YOUR** passion. Don't follow someone else's. Don't follow what someone **THINKS** you should do. Go after your dreams – *chase them down* – whatever they are. They belong to you and no one else. They were placed inside your heart, and you need to live them. We can **ADMIRE** and **RESPECT** other's abilities, talents, and successes, but imitating them is not going to result in happiness, fulfillment or success. Today you need to embrace the real you and the dreams you have for yourself.

Today's Daily Affirmation is:

I release the need to control any outcome in my life.

As humans, we have a tendency to want to control things. Of course, there's some of us who are more of a control freak than the next, but no matter what level your controlling nature is you need to stop it dead in its tracks. You cannot control much in life – but **what you can control is yourself**, your thoughts, actions, words and how you react to what happens around you. That's it. The rest belongs to God and the spiritual realm.

You can't control how other people treat you, but you can control how you treat them and respond to them. You can't control what God has planned for you, but you can control how much you trust and have faith in him. **If you can get behind the mindset of believing that every single thing that is happening in your life is for a very specific reason, you will be at peace releasing the need to control all the outcomes.**

Today's Daily Affirmation is:

I release my wants into the Universe and trust that I will be given what I need.

Sometimes we're so busy wishing for what we **"want"** we lose sight of what we may actually **"need."** I'm guilty of it, as I'm sure maybe just a few of you reading this are (*or more*)! There are times when we think we know what's best for us when God has something else in store. We can hold on to those *wants* so tight that it may actually *delay* our blessing or worse, our breakthrough.

Listen, if you understand the way the Universe works, then you know very well that eventually what is **MEANT** to happen, **will always happen**. You can take the short route or the long route and even get lost along the way, but **EVENTUALLY** (*go ahead, repeat that!*) what's **MEANT** to happen, **WILL** in fact happen. But, is there something that you've been praying for, for such a long time, something that you really **WANT** and it just hasn't come yet? If there is, then let me put this thought in your brain – perhaps **YOU** need to change what you're doing.

Maybe, just maybe you haven't been blessed with it yet because you aren't ready for it yet. Take a look at yourself – your thoughts and even your actions. You could be missing something right in front of you. That dream job you've been hoping for may just possibly be around the corner, but you need to release your hold on something else in your life first. That relationship you were hoping for a commitment out of might just not be the best thing for you right now. **Take a step back; God knows what's up, and he won't steer you wrong.** Listen, observe and breathe, it'll all fall into place just how it should in due time.

Today's Daily Affirmation is:

I will stay at peace in times of trouble and triumph.

Peace. We all crave it and for a lot of us, it's hard to obtain. Once we get it, it's hard to keep it. We were gifted with peace the moment we were born; it's ours for the keeping. But this is how negativity works – it sees something good, and it latches on. Just like it sees something bad and it latches on. It tries to bring down what's already down and wants to destroy what is good.

Spiritual battles seep into reality far more than most want to acknowledge. **We're fighting battles everyday – be it in our minds or hearts** – you might not be able to see them, but they're happening. If you aren't directly involved, then it's God, Spirit or your Angels reminding you that they are armored up and on the battlefield for you. Yes, they all fight on your behalf. But we need to help out too and the way we do that is first understanding what is happening and then not allowing it to attack us. Remember when your mother told you not to touch the pot on the stove because it was hot. But you didn't believe her and you touched it 'just to be sure,' and got burned. You can't do that in the spiritual realm – trust me, **if you feel like you're losing your peace just when you begin to get happy** and you feel like suddenly everyone's out to get you, attack you, bring you down – it's not really them – **it's a negative spirit**. That negative spirit picked someone you would feel vulnerable with as a way to get to you. To convince you that happiness isn't real. To convince you that for the rest of your life you're going to need to be miserable.

The Devil (fear/ego) is a liar. Once you accept this and understand it, you will recognize it happening and be able to not feed into it. That's all it wants – one question in your mind, "is that true," "am I really worthless," "does he really not like me for me," "am I really going nowhere in life." Yes, that is all it takes. One sign from you that you might believe what negativity has to say and there goes your peace. It's gone quicker than you realize it. So today, read this, understand it and acknowledge that negativity wants to steal your peace, but it **belongs to you and the way you keep it safe is by never questioning its existence.**

Today's Daily Affirmation is:

I am thankful for what was, what is, and what will be.

Wake up and be thankful. Thankful that you actually woke up! Thankful that you have clean air to breathe and you can see the sunshine. Be thankful for the roof over your head and the fact you can place your feet on the ground and walk without hesitation. Give thanks for your loved ones, your children, your friends, your relatives and your fur-babies.

Often we take the small things for granted. We just need to remind ourselves that even though we're not where we might want to be yet (*key word!*), **we need to be thankful for where we are, because we've come so far from where we've been.** If your day, week or even month doesn't seem to be going as planned, just remember that it could always be worse. Give thanks for the mistakes that take place and the misfortunes that happen because they are still leading you somewhere wonderful. **Be thankful that you have a powerful universal energy working for you and not against you. Be thankful for your life – it's sweet, precious and magical and it could be gone tomorrow.**

Today's Daily Affirmation is:

I refuse to lose hope.

Don't give up! Life can turn around in a split second. You know it's happened in the past and it will happen again. Don't lose faith because things don't seem to be going your way. **Everything has a reason and everything has its purpose.** Rejection is often protection. **What you feel may be pulling you back, may be preparing you to launch forward into something better.** Don't lose hope – remind yourself that everything will fall into place the way it should, when it should and you will realize why everything that took place did, in due time.

Today's Daily Affirmation is:

I promise to show love to all and accept it back in my life always.

Love is a universal language and more importantly a Universal energy. **There can be nothing without love.** You can try to argue that statement, but it's only going to lead you to the same conclusion.

Today, instead of jumping to a conclusion, getting annoyed too quickly or creating an argument, try to express love (*yes, even if it's not immediately being expressed to you*.). Be it in your eyes, thoughts, your words or your actions and the trick is to give that love to YOU first and allow it to extend outward. Because sometimes we can't imagine how we would even begin to give love to someone who perhaps upset us or even hurt us**. The trick is to offer up that love inward first. Give love and watch how it is returned to you tenfold.**

Today's Daily Affirmation is:

I release whatever is holding me back.

Do yourself a favor today and let go of what isn't serving you anymore. It could be a feeling or bad habit – a relationship, friend, or even a continuous thought process that you can't seem to break. *It's time to let it go and break free from its restraints.* How far has it gotten you so far? In order to see change, we need to change. **If you keep doing what you're doing, you'll keep getting what you got.** In order to see a different result, you need to alter something about the way you're going about it.

Today's Daily Affirmation is:

I recognize negativity's sneaky ways and refuse to let it affect me.

Have you ever noticed that we often feel the most stressed, scared or fearful right before we're about to have a major breakthrough? It's true – the Devil works overtime when he knows you're about to be blessed – to deter you as a last ditch effort. It usually doesn't work, especially if you recognize it.

However, it is hard not to feed into it because you see, we're usually blessed after we've gone through a spiritual transformation. Or when we've finally learned a lesson God has been trying for years to teach us. Or when we've finally released the "old" in our lives. **Those vibes you instantly get of wanting to give up are just negativity trying to stop your blessing.** Don't allow them to affect you. Surround yourself with a bubble of protection and cast them out. **Reclaim your peace and watch as your miracle unfolds.**

Today's Daily Affirmation is:

I acknowledge there is always something to be thankful for.

There are just going to be days when we struggle. Be it mentally, physically or emotionally. Sometimes it's something serious and other times we just can't seem to get out of our own way. Whichever it may be there is a solution to overcoming the struggle and keeping a healthy mindset. **Find what you are grateful for.** Make a list of everything that you're grateful for today. Don't write down what's bothering you, hurting you, upsetting you. **Simply write down the blessings surrounding you.** I promise you when you start observing all the good that has come your way it'll not only outweigh the bad; it'll make the bad seem so much more insignificant that you'll wonder why you wasted so many minutes dwelling on it.

Today's Daily Affirmation is:

I refuse to worry.

God is not going to give what belongs to you to someone else. Yes, we make our choices and have free will, and that might alter the route to our divine destiny, but it won't change the ending. What's meant to be will be.

If something's going to happen, it'll happen regardless of whether you're worrying about it or not. Worrying is something we all do. It's a human emotion, and the majority of us can't help it because, as humans, we want and cling to some form of control. **When we sense we're losing control, we worry.** But the funny thing about worrying is it doesn't change anything, and it only makes the waiting process longer and more dreadful. Worrying makes us miserable.

What if you could live in peace when something wasn't going the way you wanted? Wouldn't that be wonderful? You can – trust me, you can! I never thought it was possible either – but I'm not going to lie, I too, do worry. Sure, not as much as I used to – actually significantly less than I used to but I do catch myself at times. You **either let worry take over, or you take charge of worrying.** That's the trick. If you can control the *'worry'* in your brain, then you can be at peace even in times of trial and tribulation. *How exactly do you control it?* I could probably write pages about that, but the short version is to **RECOGNIZE** that it's there. You see, worry doesn't knock on your door and allow you the respect of looking through the peephole. Worry comes in – yup, it just walks right in. Sometimes worry is in disguise as the *'solution'*. Sometimes worry can convince you that it has all the answers. Don't believe it! Recognize it's there and demand that it leave. That's all. **Ask for peace and when you ask, you shall receive.**

Today's Daily Affirmation is:

No matter where I go in life I will remain humble.

You can be smart, intelligent, a genius, a master at something but you still must be humble. Being humble doesn't counteract your intelligence, but it simply means that you acknowledge there's always something more to learn. **It means that you recognize that there are people from all walks of life that can teach you something.**

There have been days where I've learned more from the mail lady then I did from a college professor. I've acquired more insight from people who haven't even graduated high school and sometimes the most innocent creatures such as animals or children can teach you the most about life. **It doesn't matter someone's title or status because that doesn't distinguish their wisdom** – however society might try at times to convince us otherwise, I'm here to tell you it's simply not true. So today humble yourself and speak to someone you wouldn't normally speak to and enjoy the lessons they have to offer you.

Today's Daily Affirmation is:

I will pay attention to the Universal signs guiding me.

You know that saying, "**When life gives you lemons, make lemonade**"? *Then why are so many people trying to make grape juice with lemons?* Listen, **you can lead a horse to water, but you can't make them drink.** (*Yes, I promise that's the last proverbial phrase I use today*). So many people are trying to get somewhere and claiming they don't know where to go, yet the directions are right in front of them. They're clearly mapped out in red Sharpie with every twist and turn while the destination is circled brightly in ink – but they refuse to acknowledge it.

Until you acknowledge what's right in front of you, you're never going to be able to get anywhere. The answers are clearly written out. The guidance is overwhelming, but you are refusing to see and hear it. Open your eyes (*they are there to see!*). Listen with your ears (*you'll be amazed at what you hear*). Follow your heart (*it doesn't steer you wrong. EVER.*).

Today's Daily Affirmation is:

I will look at things differently.

"**If you change how you look at something, the thing you look at changes.**" Dr. Wayne Dyer said this and it's a pretty powerful statement. **If you change how you view a negative situation, you might just find the positive in it.** If you change how you look at someone you feel hates you, you might just learn they don't hate you at all. They just dislike themselves. If you change how you view a failed attempt at a job, you might just find that the door was closed so a better one could open.

Today's Daily Affirmation is:

I will always give kindness so I will receive kindness in return.

Life always comes full circle. The people that once let you down will need to rely on you one day. The people that refused to help you will need your help at some point. Or it could go the other way – the people that helped you, you'll be able to pay back in the future in some form. Regardless of the circumstances, it'll all come full circle.

What goes around, comes around and vice versa. Let this be an important lesson for us all – we've all had moments of disappointment or discouragement, doubt or fear. We've all been talked down to or belittled by another human being at some point or another. Don't let it deter you and do not let it shape your character. If someone speaks poorly to you, it's usually a reflection of themselves. Don't take it personally and never take it to heart – be kind and remember they will eat those harsh words one day, and the Universe will put you in a position to witness it, I suggest you be kind then as well. **Treat everyone you encounter with the love, kindness, and respect you want and it'll always return it to you, tenfold.**

Today's Daily Affirmation is:

I am always aware of the energy I give and the energy I take.

It's interesting how energy works. You need to deal with it cautiously and be aware that where there's good, there's bad. Not to get all new age on you for a second but if the positive vibes are flowing, the negative ones are sitting in the corner waiting for a moment to attack. I'm sure I've said this before and I'll be saying it plenty more because it's important – **check your energy**. Be careful what you let in and what you let out. Be alert that at any second negative energy can strike. You could be experiencing a beautiful moment and just as it passes, *boom*, negativity finds its hole, digs in and 'tries' to ruin the moment that you just had. But if you are able to recognize it when it strikes, it'll lose its power over you (*perhaps not over the other person*) but as long as 1 person doesn't feed into it – (*remember the saying... it takes two to tango*) – well if you walk away from it, it's stuck in a dead-end and it'll eventually dissipate.

Today's Daily Affirmation is:

I am a magnet for miracles.

Do you know what a miracle is made of? It's when you finally match your energy with your divine energy. **It becomes a magnetic force that no one can stop.** On Earth, we see it as something infinitely impossible suddenly happening, but spiritually your soul *'knew'*, believed, and sent out that signal to the Universe – the Universe matched its frequency and sent it right back to you.

Energy is magnetic and very powerful. You are full of miracles just waiting to burst; it's just up to you to match up the pieces. They're all placed in front of us, scattered of course, but along our path and just like an Easter Egg hunt you must collect all the ones that belong to you and place them in your basket. Believe in what they're there for and watch some crazy things happen!

Today's Daily Affirmation is:

I will focus my attention on my blessings and be thankful.

When you get frustrated, lost, or confused, do me a favor – better yet, do yourself a favor – write down everything that you ever asked/prayed for that you received so far. **You'll soon realize that God is always listening.** He responds best to gratitude so if you're going to keep saying *"I never get an answer when I pray"* or *"why does everything bad always happen to me,"* you better check yourself.

Everything bad does not happen to you, it only feels that way if you focus on the bad. If you start focusing on the good, despite the bad, you'll notice that a lot of good things happen to you all the time. Nowadays people sit on social media a lot during the days and nights looking at other people's photos, tweets, status updates, etc. Their body's fill with jealousy and envy and think, *"what am I doing wrong?"* "Why does so-and-so always have such wonderful things happening to them?" The answer is simple – **they don't dwell on the bad. They don't dwell on the unfortunate circumstances that are always going to come and go for as long as you live.** They look at the beauty in everything. They enjoy what each day has to offer, and they are grateful for it.

Today's Daily Affirmation is:

My emotions are contagious; I will share my laughter and smile with all those in need.

Laughter truly is a natural medicine. I can only hope that no matter what you deal with during your days and nights, that you find the time to smile and laugh. It heals the soul and fills it with joy.

You might feel like you have nothing to smile about some days – but that couldn't be further from the truth. **Just as we should take time every day to find something to be thankful for, we should take time every day to find something to smile about.** Essentially these two go hand-in-hand. Laughter is so much more than just an action or emotion. **Laughter heals.** The energy that is created from it can heal you from ailments, illnesses, sadness, depression, anxiety. It's also contagious.

Go ahead, test it out...try it on your friends and family. **The important thing is that a smile can not only brighten up your day, but it can brighten someone else's.** So perhaps you can't muster up the energy to find a reason to make yourself laugh or smile – find someone else to do it for – but I warn you, prepare yourself – because it'll light up your life too!

Today's Daily Affirmation is:

I will allow the Universe to work for me and not against me.

As humans we struggle believing in things we can't see. We crave proof. We want evidence. That's alright and sometimes even understandable. **Having faith in anything is a hard task.** You have that voice in your head telling you to wholeheartedly believe, while the Devil on your shoulder is telling you not to be a fool.

Are you struggling with holding on to your faith? It doesn't matter what you believe in – you could simply be believing in yourself yet struggling to do so. **The Universe has your back in all that you do. All you have to do is ask and you will always receive.** It's that simple. No, you don't even need to be spiritual to do this. The Universe is your friend. It's energy, and energy responds to energy. Ask for confirmation and you'll get it. Ask for clarification and it will be given to you.

Today's Daily Affirmation is:

I will be still. I will have faith.

There are times in life where you just feel stagnant. The tide has calmed and you're just floating around with no waves in sight. It wasn't too long ago I felt this too. Honestly, it goes in cycles for all of us. We're all ebbing and flowing through the waters of life and suddenly the sea calms and we're just treading in one spot. **You are prepared to sit still. If you are there, that is where you are supposed to be.** All the lessons prior to this exact time, lead you to this moment of being still, being patient, and staying strong. Keep your head above water, don't give up and have faith God will see you though.

Today's Daily Affirmation is:

I release my need to control everything and trust everything to fall into place as it should.

Even if you have it all together, you are always going to go through trials and tribulations. Even if your spiritual connection is on point, your job is perfect, everyone in your family is happy and healthy, you are going to go through something. A lot of people steer away from believing in anything – any Higher Power or outside force at all because they think to themselves, *"What's the point in believing if I'm still going to have to suffer in life?"*

Yes, even if you believe in God, Buddha, the Universe or any type of God or Higher Power, you are still going to go through things – sadness, defeat, death, struggle, frustration, etc. **You will go through hard times. It is guaranteed whether you believe or not.** The difference that believing in something bigger than yourself makes is that going through a hard time becomes easier because you understand and comprehend that you are not in control.

That's also one of the main reasons why people don't want to believe – they fear losing control. They like telling themselves that it's their decisions that brought them to this point and it's up to them to get them out. Here's the thing – it **IS** your decisions which lead you to this point – but if you rely on something bigger, those decisions are easier to make. It's also less likely you'll make the **"wrong"** one (if you believe there's a wrong one) – **however I truly believe there are no mistakes in life. Everything and every choice you make has lead you to this very moment and you are in this very moment for good reason.** That reason will show itself in due time. So if you're struggling, if you're fighting through something or for something, if you're going through anything – why don't you give it up to God, the Universe, Allah, the Angels, Jehovah, Yahweh, Buddha, whomever. **Release that tight grip you've got on it and watch how it all suddenly and miraculously falls into place (as it should).**

Today's Daily Affirmation is:

No one can steal my inner peace.

It becomes really difficult with the day-to-day grind to maintain our inner peace. Inner peace is only something you can give yourself – it does not come from outside forces. **Inner peace is an understanding that no matter what takes place during your days, nothing happened by accident and everything will eventually make sense.** Energy vampires (*as so many like to call them these days*) will try to steal your peace. They can only succeed if you allow them to. You cannot let outside forces affect your inner well-being – stress will always exist, but you don't need to let it steal your peace. **If you can keep calm through the storm, the sun will shine brighter when it comes out.**

Today's Daily Affirmation is:

I receive my guidance when I'm still and I listen.

Try to find time every day to meditate. If you don't "meditate," then the way I coach my clients if they're not into that is to just sit and be still in silence. **Listen to your thoughts.** I say "your thoughts" so they can better understand what is happening, but in reality it's your intuition and speaking spiritually, it's God or your Angels speaking with you.

You see, prayer is talking to God but meditation is allowing God to speak to you, guide you, provide you with insight and wisdom into situations in your life. I get so much guidance when I meditate that to this day it still amazes me how much I'm told simply by meditating. **That is what takes place when you allow time for God every day.** That feeling of being lost or confused totally vanishes because he tells you what to do. He tells you how to handle it – whatever *'it'* may be. So even if you're not *"into"* any of this crazy *"new age"* stuff as I hear some people say (*even though it's not new age at all and has been around for centuries but society seems to be finally 'catching on'*). Even if you have absolutely no idea how to begin meditating or "talking" to God. **Find 30 minutes today to sit alone, be quiet, be still and listen. I promise you'll get the answers you're looking for.**

Today's Daily Affirmation is:

I embrace those from my past as they have lessons for my future.

Your past is not meant to haunt or harm you. Your past, and those you've encountered throughout it, were your teachers for your future. Some individuals from your past will pop up again in your future, some will not. **Former friends, ex-lovers, and even family members or strangers were placed along your journey to teach you.** *Life is one big classroom and everything we do, see, and experience are the lessons.* Recognize them so that you can continue moving forward along your journey.

Today's Daily Affirmation is:

My strategy is to be patient and stay focused on that which benefits me.

As always my pastor inspires me. I had given specific advice to a client and as I listened I realized he was speaking the same words. Keep your focus on that which benefits you. Don't get caught up in the distractions of life. Learn to wait on God because you will mature through waiting on him. Sometimes you need to be strategic to survive. **Sometimes it's strategic to keep quiet, absorb the insults thrown your way, and pick the battle that we can win.** Don't take everything personally and don't be so sensitive. Some things you need to absorb, take in, interpret, translate, and create a strategy. Recycle those words and turn them into fuel to win your battle.

Today's Daily Affirmation is:

I will become what I believe.

We become what we believe. Everything we have ever done can be traced back to what we believe. What you allow into your mind will manifest into your reality. Yes, it's true, anything – try it! No, I didn't promise it'll happen overnight like magic – however, it could in a surprisingly miraculous way. I've done it, so I know that you can do it too. **If you can wake up every morning and affirm something positive for your day, you're already setting yourself up for success.**

Today's Daily Affirmation is:

I choose to flow with the current not against it as that is where I will find peace.

Balance is ever-evolving and something we should always be seeking in our lives. The key to maintaining balance in your life is being open to accepting change gracefully, as that is where you will find peace. Yes, they all work hand-in-hand.

I was always one of those people who hated change. *Yes, hated!* The thought of it literally pissed me off to the core. However, I finally realized the longer I fight it the more the Universe is going to toss my way. **So I learned to flow with it.** That doesn't mean the Universe stops changing things in your life – it just means that I am now able to flow with the current instead of against it; and if you've ever literally tried that, then you know how difficult it is. Definitely not impossible, but a lot more difficult than letting the current push you.

My job is to work with the body as a whole – mind, body and spirit. That is the key to finding peace and balance in your life – allowing your mind, your body and your spirit to work together as one. **Don't fight the changes that come your way in any realm, flow with them, as they are happening for a purpose.**

Today's Daily Affirmation is:

I will not let negative thinking consume me. I am in control of my own thoughts.

You are going to have days where even when you are trying your best to exude positive energy, subconsciously you are freaking out. *Have you ever had that happen?* **On the outside you're calm, but on the inside there are a million questions, doubts, fears, worries.** It's important that we learn how to silence that subconscious chatter. The *'mind chatter'*, as I like to call it, is actually more powerful then we realize.

You see the Universe picks up on that banter in our brains. God hears us, even if we are not speaking it out loud. *So how exactly do we hit the mute button on those worries in our mind?* Trust that all will be well and work out for the highest good of everyone involved. Affirm that you are in control of your own thoughts and that you release all questions to God and the Universe and believe they will all be answered at the right moment.

Today's Daily Affirmation is:

I believe that nothing happens by accident and everything happens for a reason.

There are going to be occasions (*a lot of them!*) when things do not turn out the way you would have hoped. Don't let it deter you. Don't let it frustrate you or even anger you. It's very easy to feel these emotions when something doesn't go our way or even just the way we prayed it would. What we all (*yes, even myself*) need to understand is that though **it might not have gone the way we had wished, it went the way it was supposed to go.** Nothing is ever out of order and nothing ever happens by accident. Trust me on this – if you don't get the reason revealed to you immediately why what took place did, it will unfold down the road. You'll look back at it and say, ***"now it all makes complete sense!"***

Today's Daily Affirmation is:

I am comforted knowing that even though it hasn't happened yet, it will happen in due time.

Just because something doesn't take place on "our" time, doesn't mean it's not going to happen. Spiritual time is way different then the time we keep here in the physical realm. **God has perfect timing for everything in your life.** When you get that dream job, when you go through a breakup, when you meet that special someone and even right down to when you're running late for an appointment and your car doesn't start.

You can look at things as having "good luck" or "bad luck" or you can look at them as *'there's a really good reason for this taking place in my life right now and eventually it'll be revealed to me why.'* **Because the truth is that it WILL eventually be revealed to you in due time – that means at the right time, at the time you need to know.** So trust the process, take what the Universe has to offer and believe that God has a time, a place and a meaning for every single thing in your life.

Today's Daily Affirmation is:

I have faith in myself.

Doubt is one of those emotions that we all experience at some point in our lives and a lot of us feel it weekly, if not daily. We doubt circumstances, we doubt people, we doubt ourselves. Doubt can be so powerful that it'll cause us to fear and worry. **It'll make us think things and tell ourselves stuff that isn't necessarily true.** Here's the thing about doubt though – because it's so powerful it can actually change the outcome of a situation.

Doubt is the opposite of faith and faith is the substance of things hoped for but not yet seen. Faith is a strong belief or trust in something or someone. **Believing in things that we don't have the evidence of seeing yet.** So when you doubt a person or a situation, your fears usually end up being true. You've placed that worry out into the Universe and shifted the energy into a negative direction. But when you have faith – sometimes the energy may take a while, but you're shifting things not only in a positive direction – you're shifting them to align with what's on your heart. *Faith begins with you.* Trust your heart, your intuition and your feelings.

Today's Daily Affirmation is:

I promise to only give out what I want to receive back.

What you give is what you get in return. People are not always going to reciprocate that kindness or generosity that you put out, but put it out there anyway. **The right ones will return it to you at the right time.**

Remember that when you seek revenge or you practice hatred – it may not be returned immediately, but it'll find its way back to you. Yes, every single thing you do – from the words you speak, the texts you send to your posts on Facebook. Before you act, think to yourself... *would I want this done to me?'* Then think to yourself, *'if this travels back around, will I like what happens to me?'* If the answers are **'No'** then it is best you rethink your words/actions.

Today's Daily Affirmation is:

I will not stress or panic if things don't go my way. The Universe is in complete control of everything.

When situations don't seem to be going your way the first thing we usually want to do is panic. But once we realize we have no control over most situations, then we can sit back and let God and the Universal powers handle it for us. **The situation is going to turn out for the best of all involved in the end, so there is no reason for us to stress or let our emotions take over.** If we can keep our mind right and stay focused on the truth of it all, we'll be able to remain at peace no matter what comes our way.

Today's Daily Affirmation is:

I will release the old, as it no longer serves me and I will welcome the new with excitement.

In order for us to grow, we need to leave some things behind to make room for what's new. Just as a young child outgrows his shoes every few months, always needing a new pair – we outgrow habits, emotions, friendships, relationships...even jobs or dreams. You'll always have memories of these things, but as humans we have a tendency to cling so tight, not wanting to let go. **We hold on to them which leaves no room for the new that's ready and waiting to enter our lives.** Spend a moment today to review something you're clinging to. Something that may not be serving you anymore. Something you've outgrown. Sure, you may *'miss'* it, just as we miss a childhood friendship or that cute pair of shoes that no longer fit our size 8 feet. **But I promise what's waiting for you is so much better.**

Today's Daily Affirmation is:

I will live each day believing I've done the very best I could in each moment.

Guilt is a hard emotion to rid yourself of. It comes when we feel we could have done more. It arises when we empathize or even sympathize with someone. Everyone experiences guilt. I'm not sure there's a way to not feel it, but **it's important we learn how to not hold onto it. It's not an emotion to lock away inside of ourselves because it acts as a virus – it slowly destroys from the inside, out.**

Just as we were not given the spirit of fear from God, we were not given the spirit of guilt. Each day we wake up and that is a blessing. We should be thankful. Now that we were given that day, we should give our best to everyone and everything we encounter. That is all we can do. We are humans, we make mistakes because none of us are perfect. **All we can do is ask for forgiveness, forgive ourselves, and move forward knowing we did all we could do with what we knew in that moment – trusting that God will take care of the rest.** Today release any guilt you've got on the inside. *Let it go!*

Today's Daily Affirmation is:

I will keep my mind strong, grateful, and positive.

Life is one big mental challenge. When your mind is on point everything seems to follow suit and fall into place. **When you can wake up, set your intentions and keep a positive attitude throughout your day no matter what happens – then you're on your way to success (even if you don't feel it).**

Your mind is a powerful weapon and tool. You can use it to your advantage or it can be used against you. The goal is to never have your own mind turn on you. When it tries, you need to recognize it and put a stop to it immediately before it gets the best of you. Even I have mental battles at times – matter of fact, everyone does once in a while. Sometimes you may feel like allowing it to win because it's too much effort to fight it. Don't give in to those negative thoughts or habits. **Today I want you to set an intention that every time something negative seeps into your brain, you will stop and think of something you are grateful for.** Replace the negative with a positive each time and watch the miracles unfold.

Today's Daily Affirmation is:

I expect miraculous things to unfold from every curveball thrown in my path.

You know the saying, *"when one door closes, another one opens"*? As hard as it is to hear people say catchy little phrases like this when you're upset, hurt, confused, etc., this one has a lot of truth in it. **Sometimes God has to literally take things away from us to make room for something else.** At the time you may not understand. At the time you may simply just want to remain mad. **But we need to not allow our emotions to get the best of us.** You see, while we're sitting around being frustrated or angry at the fact we got laid off from our job, we might miss a dream opportunity staring us right in the face.

They also say, *"God works in mysterious ways,"* right? He does – **he also has a great sense of humor. So we need to learn to maintain ours when life throws us unwarranted curve-balls** – because there is a rhyme and a reason for it all. Eventually, it'll all come together like a jigsaw puzzle and every uphill battle, and downhill slope will make complete sense. Until then, laugh at the confusion and roll with the punches – the Universe only has our best interest at heart.

Today's Daily Affirmation is:

I allow faith to fill me up, leaving no room for my doubts, worries, or fears.

Doubt cannot be present in our lives if we have faith. These two do not mix – ever! If you doubt something – anything; a relationship, situation, job, any opportunity in general, then you cannot have faith in it. Doubt is like a disease. To quote Emily Thorne from ABC's *Revenge*: *"Doubt is a disease. It infects the mind, creating a distrust of people's motives and of one's own perceptions. Doubt has the ability to call into question everything you've ever believed about someone. And reinforce the darkest suspicions of our inner circles."*

You are betting against yourself when you doubt what you believe in, whom you believe in or the situations you believe in. The power of the mind is such that when you place that stamp of doubt upon something, it is branded – tainted – and it's best just to release it from your mind at that point before the doubt spreads. So if there's something you're working towards, something you're hoping for, or simply something you are trying to draw into your life – allow faith to fill you up and leave no room for doubt.

Today's Daily Affirmation is:

I am full of infinite possibilities.

We are in a Universe full of infinite possibilities. But we are narrow thinkers. We don't realize the power of our abilities, sometimes until it's too late. **We have the ability to access a world of opportunity – anything you want, you can have.** The problem is that we doubt the things we wish for. *How do you plan on accessing all these wonderful things when as soon as you release the belief into the Universe, you're swatting it right back down?* **You are making these endless possibilities, impossible to get.** We need to overcome our narrow thinking and realize that we are full of potential – matter of fact, we're born with it. The only way we can get everything we want in our lives is for us to believe we can.

Today's Daily Affirmation is:

I stay humble and let my actions speak louder than my words.

Having too much pride is poison to your soul. Pride does nothing for you other than destroy any opportunity you have offered to you. Unfortunately, a lot of people these days feel as if having pride is a good thing. They think it represents confidence and success. This is false thinking. Pride does the opposite. It shows you are insecure with your knowledge and talents. It proves you hold resentment and stubbornness towards not only yourself but other people as well.

Humility is what attracts success into your life. Humility stems from being grateful for your opportunities that were gifted to you on your path. Humility is the only remedy for that bottle of poison you've been drinking labeled **"pride"**. Instead of boasting about the things you've done in life, allow your talents and accomplishments to speak for themselves. **Allow your actions to speak louder than your words.** This is how you advance along your journey. **The humblest of people are the most successful – and you never hear about half of what they've achieved** – they do good and persevere for the sake of doing good without needing the acknowledgement and reassurance that those with pride seek after. And that's simply because they provide themselves internally with the recognition that one with pride is seeking externally!

Today's Daily Affirmation is:

I am not lacking anything; for I have all I need within me.

"It's all in your head" comes across like such a negative, hurtful term – but the truth is, it is all in our heads! **You ever feel like you're waiting for something 'big' to happen and that 'thing' will bring you such joy.** That *'thing'* will fulfill you and make your life complete? That *'thing'* that so many of us long for, doesn't exist. Yes…I know, I'm sorry that's disappointing to read, but it's all in your head.

That *'thing'* is a lack in our own thinking. We're not giving ourselves enough credit. **We are already fulfilled with everything we need in this moment. Those extras that we're longing for are just cherries on top.** If we feel like we are *'lacking'* something that is going to complete us, that is the time you stop and look within. **Are you not being grateful for where you are right this very second and what you have?** Don't misunderstand me, it's wonderful to dream and hope and *WANT* more for ourselves. We can want anything at all – there's nothing wrong with that. **The truth is we can have it all too! But, right now, in this very moment – you shouldn't feel like something that you don't have yet is the answer to your happiness.**

The answer to your own happiness is already inside of you. As time moves, we grow, develop and change and moment by moment we will be gifted with everything our heart desires – because when the time comes that you are given it, you will be *READY* for it. **But if you don't have it yet – you are not ready for it.** This is the time you search within yourself and find the reason you're feeling this way, because there's an important lesson there. It's the key to unlocking the desires of your heart.

Today's Daily Affirmation is:

I will be where I am in this moment.

Gabrielle Bernstein will often say "Don't get caught up in future-tripping." What she means is staying where you are in the present moment rather than jumping ahead to the future. I'm very guilty of doing this as I'm sure a lot of you out there are. Sometimes we find ourselves day-dreaming about future events. Not in a negative way, but in a hopeful way with a confident spirit knowing *'it'll happen'* at the right time. The problem is that if we are sitting there placing our minds in the future, we're missing the present – and the present is exactly where we need to be right now.

Be where you are! When we are **"future-tripping"** Gabby explains, **we cut off the energy flow.** We need to fully participate in *'this'* moment and at the right time we will be guided in the right direction. Today I want us all to keep our minds in this moment and if you catch yourself "future-tripping" turn yourself right back around into the present moment and the best way I find to do that is to ask yourself, "What am I doing right now?" It automatically redirects your attention to whatever is right in front of you this moment.

Today's Daily Affirmation is:

Today, I am grateful for the "hard stuff".

Good days and bad days are going to happen regardless of our financial status, degrees and titles we hold or even how in love we are. Bad days will happen no matter how positive you are; No matter how good your relationship with God is. "Nobody ever said it would be easy," right? **We were never promised an easy life, but we were promised peace and joy amidst the storm.**

Sometimes our bad days are merely a result of our own doing. We get caught up in our own head-space even though we know better. It's days like that, that make it difficult for us to accept we don't have control over everything. That **there's a larger plan in action for us – a better one that has our highest good at its forefront.** *The best way to conquer days like that, remind ourselves that the hard stuff reveals the good stuff.* The blocks are for protection. The endings are to advance us into something better. The frustrations are there to teach us about ourselves. It's all for your highest good.

Today's Daily Affirmation is:

I control my circumstances by supervising my emotions.

It's common to allow our circumstances to affect our feelings; to change our mood. It's difficult however, to allow our emotions to determine our circumstances. But that is in fact what happens. *Ever notice how if you start letting the small things upset you in the morning; spilled coffee, ran out of the cereal you like, someone mowing their lawn extra early – then your whole day tends to unravel and almost everything pisses you off?* That's because we let the events of the morning determine how the rest of our day is going to go. But if we flip that and reverse it and set the tone for our day no matter our situations, and allow that to be the determining factor – **we will set ourselves up for success and inner peace and it simply won't matter what's happening around us.**

Today's Daily Affirmation is:

I do not resist the Universal teachings in my life.

Sometimes a lesson was trying to be taught to us for years, but it takes us being told by someone else or reading it in a different context to really grasp and fully learn it. I'm not sure why that happens the way it does, but our brains all operate differently. I'm a very visual person – be it pictures, words or actions, I learn better when I see things. Some people understand better by just listening. We're all different, but like I said **we're all connected in this Universe. Today I want you to reflect on something that you notice repeating in your life.** *Do you continue to hear the same words being spoken to you by different individuals?* Are you noticing people reacting to things you do/say the same way? Maybe there is no current pattern, but there once was. This is God/Universe's way of trying to *'breakthrough'* to you. **There is a lesson in this.** Reflection is an important part of spiritual growth, and the only way we can advance into new endeavors, situations and relationships in life is if we focus on our personal growth.

Today's Daily Affirmation is:

I am full of love and will express kindness to everyone, no matter what.

During moments of anger, we sometimes feel the need to attack. To point out someone else's flaws or fears and rub them in their face. *But do we really like that when it's done to us?* Most likely the answer is no.

Treating others how we want to be treated is sometimes easier said than done. Especially during heated moments when your brain clouds and the words fly out of your mouth without thinking. It happens to the best of us. **But what we put out is always returned to us – so if we're putting out anger, rage or even cattiness, we'll receive that in return.**

Gossip; it comes back to us. Hate; expect it wrapped with a nice big bow. **It's the hard road to take to express love towards individuals we may not be fond of.** Not love in the sexual sense – love as in a deep respect for them as a person, no matter who they are or what they've done or gone through. **We cannot judge books by their cover and we cannot and should not fight fire with fire when it comes to other humans.** Treat them as you would like to be treated, in every situation. It's the tough thing to do, but you never know what that person's been through, what they're battling or why they maybe are so mean. You have no idea, so **just express love and let God handle the drama.**

Today's Daily Affirmation is:

I am capable of manifesting anything I desire.

Planetary shifts and energy patterns happen every second of every day and at any moment we can fully step into a new one. Focus on the excitement that brings. That at any moment you can have a breakthrough, an epiphany or a miracle. **Expecting it will put your dreams and desires into motion.**

I was reading a book and it explained it perfectly like this (*I'm summarizing here in my own words): Our thoughts are energy. Think of them like a battery. A battery standing alone is full of energy just waiting to be used. But the energy cannot be accessed until you put it into something to activate the energy. Place the battery into a stereo and the energy is now Kinetic. It's in motion. It's what makes the stereo play. This is SCIENCE my friends! Our thoughts, actions and words work the same way. We can manifest anything we want into our life by thinking, speaking, writing or doing. The more emotion we place behind it, the quicker it's able to manifest. But if we put no action behind these, it's as if we're the battery without the stereo. We're full of possibility but can't do anything with it.*

You can say you want something and you can get on your knees every single night and pray for it and God-willing in due time you may receive it **BUT if you make an intention to not only hope for it, but to take the right steps towards getting it, you are guaranteed it.**

Today's Daily Affirmation is:

I choose to give love with no ulterior motive.

Showing and giving love is a beautiful thing. Being a selfless human being and truly caring for others is not just the "right" thing to do but it's what we all should be doing. There's one problem, however, and that's that a lot of us feel we can change people. **We are only responsible for ourselves and our words, thoughts, and actions.** We cannot 'make' other people be a certain way, think a certain way, act a certain way, etc.

The biggest most crucial part of my job is to not try to change people – it's to guide them in the right direction towards their highest self. That means their best self. Whatever it is upon their heart to pursue is the direction they need to go. I am here to provide the tools and guidance, motivation and wisdom to help you get there. I cannot change you as a person though, nor do I want to. I cannot make you think the same way I do or believe the same things I believe. **We want so bad sometimes to help people, but we fool ourselves thinking we can change them.** There's a big difference between helping someone be a better person and changing them all-together. **We should never change people. We should cherish and accept them for all their beauty and imperfections.**

Today's Daily Affirmation is:

I believe everything is happening exactly how it should.

Circumstances are not always going to play out the way we think they will. You know that saying, "life happens when you're making other plans;" well it's so very true. **It's funny how when you dwell on a situation, you delay it, but when you put your energies into more productive activities – things just always seem to pan out just the way they should.**

God really does work in mysterious ways and we never really know what he is up to, but we can trust that he always has our best interests at hand when calling the shots from above. **So today if something doesn't go the way you thought it should, don't let it upset you – it's going the way it's supposed to go.** *Happy accidents – no coincidences – everything has its place and purpose;* just trust!

Today's Daily Affirmation is:

I will always respond to hate with love.

Hurt people, hurt people. It's true. Before we're quick to respond, or worse, react – we need to keep this in mind. People act out, cause pain and say mean things because they are hurt. It doesn't matter if that hurt was caused by you and now you're on the receiving end or not. It could have been created decades prior to even knowing that person, but you're receiving the tail-end of their pain. It's hard to not be affected by this. We are human beings. However, **situations will have less effect on you when you better understand why it's happening.**

You don't have to study Psychology to understand why people act the way they do. You just need to grasp this basic lesson: **if someone hurts you or comes at you the wrong way it's usually due to their own pain.** Projection is the easiest way for emotionally wounded individuals to cope. It's not right, it's never okay, but we can only be responsible for our own words and actions. So knowing this now, the next time you're in a situation that isn't exactly kosher, you can breathe instead of react because **silence is more powerful than words ever could be.** You are also demonstrating a love, understanding and a valuable lesson for another human being when you allow them that space to feel their pain they've just tried to place on you.

Today's Daily Affirmation is:

I find the answers when I am centered and grounded.

We all know better sometimes, *don't we?* **The answers are usually directly under our nose and instead of paying attention we let our minds take over and overwhelm us.** That's when things spiral out of control. Thoughts begin to emerge like *"what am I doing wrong,"* or *"I have no idea what to do now, nothing is working the way it should."*

These thoughts are self-deprecating thoughts. We are undermining and doubting ourselves. When situations start to overwhelm you because they are not working out the way they should and you start questioning yourself, which then leads to questioning everything we have been doing or have done and then questioning our entire existence. This is when we need to **STOP** and ground ourselves.

When this happened to me in the past, I got so overwhelmed I started searching for methods outside of myself when really and truly I already knew the answers to my problems. **We can't allow our minds to take over during trials and tribulations.** We can't search for coping mechanisms when our mind is spatting out thoughts, fears, and self-deprecation. We know better! **We need to be mindful. We need to stop and come back to our center and ground ourselves.** That is when the answers that have been within you the entire time reveal themselves.

Today's Daily Affirmation is:

I am accessing the power within me.

We are born with strength in our hearts. It's the struggles we encounter along the way that break us down bit by bit. But you were born with an enormous amount of strength within you and it never leaves. You can tap into that strength at any time. It is at that point when you'll realize what your true potential is. It is then when you'll realize that you don't need others to give it to you.

Set an intention to access your own power today. Make up your mind to not let it sit wasted. Sometimes we are so busy looking for comfort and support elsewhere that we fail to realize we can do the same for ourselves. Our souls are powerful sources of energy that can give you the willpower and stamina for any dream you want to conquer.

Today's Daily Affirmation is:

My reality is what I perceive it to be. I can alter my reality by understanding my perception.

We are only living out our perception of what reality is. When we change how we view something, the thing changes. Altering how you view someone who consistently argues with you no matter what you do, might make you realize that the arguments have nothing to do with you at all. Perceiving someone in a different light who appears to copy your every move will help you understand that it's merely their own insecurities they are acting out. Change how you look at yourself and those feelings of lack, misconception and loneliness will fade away. **Life is a mind game.** Human nature is to react first, think later. **Once we're mindful, we learn to think first, understand our perception then act.**

Today's Daily Affirmation is:

The more positive and beautiful things I affirm, the more I see!

We are only as smart as we allow ourselves to be. We are only as motivated as we allow ourselves to be. We are only as fun, kind, and beautiful as we allow ourselves to be. **We can be our worst enemy or our best friend.**

Unfortunately, a lot of us hate on ourselves far too often – sometimes without even realizing it. I'll give you a good example – I wake up every day and even I will sit down to write these affirmations and block myself mentally. I'll start to think about whether I wrote something like this before or am I running out of topics to write about in general. As I do that to myself, it ends up taking me much longer to get the words that are on the tip of my tongue out *because I'm my worst critic.*

Criticizing my work in my head, I've blocked myself from being able to perform my work for all of you. *Now, is there something you've been trying to accomplish, participate in, or get motivated for that you're criticizing yourself about?* **Be honest with yourself** because we all do it. From the moment we look in the mirror to putting on an outfit to heading out the door, **we subconsciously affirm things to ourselves that are negative.** When you catch yourself doing this – pause and reverse your statement into a positive one. **The more you affirm the positive and beautiful things, the more positive and beautiful things you will see!**

Today's Daily Affirmation is:

I trust myself, my intuition, and my journey.

Everybody needs somebody to trust, talk to, and confide in. Even I have people I turn to when I'm in need of advice – however, *a lot of times we're so desperately seeking an answer from someone else that we fail to realize we already know what to do*. I would say about 97% of the time we already know what decision we want to make and what we should do and we seek those outside sources for confirmation.

That's ok – but **what I want to affirm today is that we need to learn to trust ourselves more.** Trust your instincts, trust your gut feelings, trust your intuition. **These tools are God-given and they do not steer you wrong.** Doubt = don't do it. Obsessing = stop. Find your peace and trust the Universe will come through as it always does. **God is always working for you, not against you.** God is making things happen even when you think you're at a stand-still. Those internal feelings are his way of communicating with us – so when our free will comes into play, we do not go and make a disaster out of things. Sure, that can still happen, but mostly when we ignore our intuition.

Today's Daily Affirmation is:

My perception of myself is what allows me to succeed or fail.

We are all one therefore we are all equal. Status hierarchy is a mere perception of ours. What those *"above"* us *"have"* is potential in us. What those *"above"* us *"earned"* is potential in us. **We are all capable of doing amazing things in our lives, but it's our own perception of ourselves that prevents that from happening.** It blocks us – stops us dead in our tracks. If you think you're rich, you are. If you think you're poor, you are. If you think you are full of possibility and can accomplish anything, you can. It is all our own perception. **Change your perception and you open up a glorious world of opportunity just waiting for you.**

Today's Daily Affirmation is:

I have the power to bring to life anything I focus my mind on.

Whatever you focus your mind on consistently, you will bring life to. *Doreen Virtue* explains that, *"Worrying is a form of prayer."* Worrying, doubting, dwelling, and fearing are all forms of prayer. You and only you have the ability to bring to life your fears as well as your dreams. That's up to you to decide. God doesn't give us the spirit of fear. He gives us the spirit of peace! We are meant to trust him with the desires of our heart. Trust means not having any fear or doubt about it taking place.

If you feel as if your prayers aren't being answered lately – *is it because your mind has been focusing on the fears?* Are you hoping for something to happen but your **"mind-chatter"** is saying *"yeah right."* **Only you can control your thoughts. Stay disciplined and have faith that everything in your heart will take place at the right time.**

Today's Daily Affirmation is:

I will speak to myself kindly because my words hold power.

Confidence has everything to do with how we perceive ourselves. You ever have those days where you wake up and you're feeling really good? You head out into the world with your head held high and a smile on your face. Towards the end of the day as you're arriving back home and feeling so good, you glance at yourself in the mirror and think, *"THAT's what I looked like all day?!"* It's happened to all of us before. Then we think, *"why didn't anyone say I looked like a hot mess or tell me that I had lipstick on my teeth?"* It was all in how you carried yourself and how you felt about yourself that day. Nobody is perfect and hardly anyone probably noticed the lipstick smudge on your teeth when you were walking around with a glowing smile and your shoulders back. **All it takes is a little negative self-talk to lead us into a downward spiral of insecurity and despair.** But **if we affirm to ourselves, "I am beautiful," "I am confident", "You can do this!" You can and you will.**

Today's Daily Affirmation is:

I forgive myself for doubting, dwelling, and fearing.

Today is the perfect time to practice your patience and forgiveness. Releasing the old and letting things go is truly what needs to happen and the best way to begin that is to forgive yourself. **Forgive yourself for 5 things that you felt you'd never get, weren't good enough to have, or didn't deserve.** *Scarce thinking is the result of fear. We fear we're not good enough so we believe we can't have what we deserve.* The truth is that we're created with all we need and we just need to believe that and release the fear to acquire it in physical form. Honestly forgiving yourself will release that fear. If we forgive ourselves for our lack mentality, we are free and whole again.

Today's Daily Affirmation is:

I believe I can, so I will.

If you have a father, be grateful. If you have a mother, be grateful. If yours have passed on or you didn't have biological parents present in your life, be grateful for the parental substitutes that stepped forward and took on that role. We choose our parents; it's not the other way around. Before we're born, our spirits select our mother's and father's, and our journeys. **These figures are in our lives to teach us lessons that we have also chosen for this lifetime.**

Many times, as children, we teach our parents a thing or two as well. *The bond is unbreakable, no matter how you feel about the relationship itself.* **Parents are meant to guide and support. To lead us and pump us full of enough knowledge that we are able to stand on our own with our heads held high and follow our heart's desires.** If you didn't have a parent or parental figure that made you believe you can do anything and be anything your heart desires, then I'm here to tell you that you can. **Sometimes the one's we love the most can tell us the things we need to hear, but it takes hearing it from a completely different place to reinforce and confirm that it's true.**

Today's Daily Affirmation is:

I will not be quick to judge.

You never know someone's struggle until you have walked in their shoes. People are fighting battles every day – mentally, emotionally, physically – and we might know nothing about it. Do not be too quick to judge or speak. **Our tongue is a powerful weapon that can be used against others as well as ourselves.** *What you speak will come back to you* though – remember that before the words leave your lips.

Today's Daily Affirmation is:

I am powerful and I will use my power for good.

We are powerful creatures and sometimes we take advantage of the power we hold and use it as a disservice to ourselves and others. Life is hard enough; we do not need to make it harder. Instead of tearing each other down, we need to learn and teach to lift each other up. Support and be kind. Be each other's cheerleaders, not enemies.

Jealously stems from fear and we were not given the spirit of fear. You do not need to live a life of jealously and anger – *you were born with your own unique gifts to offer this world.* **When you compare yourself to others, you are not acknowledging your special gifts and that is doing a disservice to yourself and your soul.**

Today's Daily Affirmation is:

I have no fears. The Universe will continue to provide for me what I need right now.

As I re-study the teaching manual for *A Course in Miracles*, I always stumble upon new concepts in the book that pop out at me. You could read something or even experience something at one point in your life and perceive it in one context. Then you could do it all over again during another time in your life and you perceive the same things completely differently. This happens daily in our lives; we just don't always pay as close attention to it happening. **We learn, we grow, and we embrace change.** Having said that, this particular part of the book read, *"...miracles are natural, corrective, healing and universal. There is nothing they cannot do, but they cannot be performed in the spirit of doubt or fear. When you are afraid of anything, you are acknowledging its power to hurt you.... You believe in what you value. If you are afraid, you are valuing wrongly."* – A Course in Miracles

If we believe we were born with all we need already within us, then common sense states that we should never be lacking. **If we think we're lacking, we're allowing that to have power over us and therefore devaluing ourselves.** I work with many different people for all different types of needs: finances, career, life, relationships, etc. Every person, me included, has our own worries or fears. Something *"more"* we are striving for. Here's the thing: we aren't lacking in anything. We don't need to be fearing anything. We may not have or be in the financial situation we'd prefer, but that does not mean we're lacking it. It means if we believe we're rich, we are. **Know that as long as you take positive steps in the right direction and believe the Universe will provide, it always does.** We believe in what we value – so if you're scared of something, you are valuing it incorrectly. *Change your thought process, change your life.*

Today's Daily Affirmation is:

I trust I will always be given what I need, not always what I want.

God will provide everything you need, exactly when you need it. Trust and believe that you will never be lacking in anything that you *"need"* (***not what you "want"***). Sometimes we mistake the things we want for the things we need. There's a big difference, and when you're in the moment of lusting and craving things, it'll be hard to differentiate.

But once you pass that moment, you'll be able to notice the right time – the time that particular thing is **NEEDED** in your life; you'll feel it deep in your soul. **When you are ready, all the things you've prayed for will be gifted to you.** Sometimes even when we think we are ready, we are not. Patience is the hardest thing to have when we think we know what is best for us, but only God and the Universe know what is best for us and what we need. We just need to trust in them wholeheartedly to always provide (*because they always do and always will*).

Today's Daily Affirmation is:

I am thankful for the signs of confirmation the Universe sends to me.

Your prayers are not going unanswered. The Universe delivers us signs of reassurance, confirmation and comfort continually throughout the day. **It's just a matter of opening your eyes and trusting yourself enough to accept them for what they are.**

It could be a word from a stranger, a comment during your favorite TV show, or even a bird perched in your window. This is the Universe's way of communicating with us. I've received endless signs from certain colored birds to random comments from complete strangers in the most unexpected places. Even something as small as signing onto social media and the first quote that pops up is as if it is speaking directly to you. These are signs, and when you acknowledge them, the Universe sends you more. **They are meant to help us maintain our peace and patience while we wait for our blessings to arrive.**

Today's Daily Affirmation is:

My love for myself is reflected in my relationships.

Our relationships are very important, but we need to realize that they are also a reflection of ourselves. If you cannot seem to get along with someone in your close circle, perhaps it's something you're identifying in them that you do not like in yourself. There is always something we can learn from every encounter, and if we aren't willing to self-reflect and do some work on ourselves, we'll never grow – personally or spiritually.

Are there traits that you simply do not like about yourself? Is there a broken relationship that you keep wishing could be fixed? **Everything can be mended and renewed if we invest the time in caring and loving ourselves first.**

Today's Daily Affirmation is:

I am happy regardless of my circumstances.

Often we feel as if until our circumstances are different, we cannot be happy. **We feel as if there's no reason to smile when we're not where we want to be in life yet.** This couldn't be further from the truth. *Joy is a gift to us.* We can access it any time we want. **Unfortunately, a lot of us believe we can't until situations change.**

Don't allow this false-thinking to steal your joy. You can have $1 to your name and still be happy because you know the Universe will provide all of your needs. You can be working a 9-5 job you are not very proud of and still be joyous because you know doors will be opened for you in due time. If we sit around waiting for certain circumstances to influence our mood, we'll always be unhappy. No one every promised an easy life. No one ever said there wouldn't be hard times or sad times. But amidst it all, you can access your God-given joy. **DESPITE** your circumstances, you can be happy. Do not feel guilty, do not doubt yourself for one second – **you're happy because you know what's coming in your life.** *If it's in your heart, it's yours – you just might not be ready for it quite yet.* So until you are, open up that gift of joy and put it to good use!

Today's Daily Affirmation is:

I love myself inside and out.

Loving yourself is the hardest most difficult thing you are ever going to have to do in life. Some of you may think *"yeah right"* or try to dispute that, but it's true. Completely loving yourself is a process and sometimes it takes years and years to get right. **When you can fully love yourself, that is when you can release the self-doubt and fear from within, you will be able to trust yourself in every situation and relationship.** You will be able to rely on your intuition without needing reassurance.

I can honestly say that my 20's were a learning and growing experience. Even looking at myself just 2 years ago, I cannot believe how far I've come. I'm not talking about achievements – *where I've gone or what I've done* – I'm talking about my relationship and love for myself. **The way you treat yourself is what sets the tone for how others treat you. The way you view the people around you is a mirror reflection of how you are viewing yourself.** If the negative is outweighing the positive, it is time to sit down and have some alone time with **'you'**. When you learn to be proud of you, enjoy your own company and know yourself inside and out and love every ounce of it – *that is when this journey gets so much easier.* The love we show for ourselves will outshine any situation that comes our way. **It will attract into our lives what needs to be there and prevent what does not from coming in.**

Today's Daily Affirmation is:

I will receive all that I need when I'm ready for it.

Answers are presented to us when we are ready to receive them – not when we **THINK** we are ready; when we **ARE** ready. **We can think one thing, but we may be another.** There are so many things, too many to count, in my life that I've prayed for time and time again while waiting patiently for an answer.

When you have felt like you have waited long enough; when you feel like you have been super patient – *this is when you need to wait longer.* **You see, when our patience runs thin, that is when we are almost there.** Just when you're about to give up and take matters into your own hands, that's when you need to stop yourself and recognize that you're **ALMOST** there. You are mere inches from your goal, and you need to just be still and wait a little bit longer.

It is like when you're waiting in that super long line for your favorite roller coaster and you really want to be in the front seat. You have already waited 20 minutes and you could easily get on next if you settle for a middle or back seat – but you **WANT** that front seat. Sometimes we just say, *"what the hell"* and we settle. But when it's something you **REALLY** want – you **WANT** to experience that ride in the very front and you've already waited those 20 minutes – what's another 5 minutes?

The things that are in your heart, they are worth the wait. If we got everything we wanted easily, it would lose its worth. *Do you take better care of the hand-me-down shoes you got from your older sister for free or the pair of shoes you spent half your paycheck on?* **We learn to appreciate things more when we have to wait for them.** We learn to cherish them and acknowledge their worth. Relationships, good friends, dream jobs – if they are handed to you on a silver platter, *would you be more inclined to take them for granted compared to something that you wanted so desperately to have and worked so hard to achieve.* Think about it! Stop, breathe and tell yourself, **"You're almost there, hold on!"**.

Today's Daily Affirmation is:

Fear does not control me.

When we are rooted in fear, we become unbalanced. Fear is self-induced and even though we create it for ourselves, we have an awfully hard time ridding ourselves of it. It's like a virus that creeps into all realms of our life and **the only way to get rid of it is to be mindful of how we brought it there in the first place.** When you grasp what brought it in, you are able to succeed in eliminating it permanently.

Today's Daily Affirmation is:

I have faith in divine right timing.

Sometimes we are continually seeking the answers to things and we feel like we're getting radio silence everywhere we turn. When we receive silence it's usually because we're not ready for the answer yet (*good or bad*). However, you know that saying, *"silence is deadly."* It is! **Silence is a real patience-tester.** If you've been praying the same prayer or asking the same questions for months and receiving nothing in response to them, stop! *Stop and let it go.*

That doesn't mean what you're asking for isn't going to happen and it also doesn't mean you'll have to live without ever getting an answer – it just means it's not TIME yet. Our time and divine timing are two completely different things. God's time is not actual time as we know it. It is where we are along our individual journeys. **If we haven't learned an important lesson yet that we need to learn BEFORE this particular thing takes place – then it's not TIME yet.** If we have not overcome something, achieved something or been introduced to the right people yet prior to what we are asking for – it's probably not **TIME** yet.

Trust divine timing! Let God be God – he knows what's up – he knows exactly what he's doing. We don't understand it 99.9% of the time and we're not meant to – we're meant to trust. **We need to understand that even when we are receiving silence, there is A LOT going on behind the spiritual scenes that we have no clue about.** We're being set up and placed in position for things we couldn't even imagine. **Hold tight, be strong, have faith and be patient – you'll get what you're seeking at exactly the RIGHT TIME!**

Today's Daily Affirmation is:

I will stay present.

Don't invest your time and energy into doubts. Instead, invest your full energy into this moment right now. **When you allow your mind to wander, you are giving negativity an opportunity to snatch its attention.** But if you can stay completely involved in this moment right now, you'll not only keep the energy balanced – but you're also allowing it to flow naturally the way the Universe wants it to. That means those blessings and miracles can happen sooner **because you aren't investing any energy into worrying about them happening.**

Today's Daily Affirmation is:

I fight my battles with love.

You never know the battles someone else is fighting in their life. They could appear whole on the outside and be torn and broken on the inside. **We can't judge a book by its cover and sometimes we can't even judge it by what it shares with us.** Sometimes you just need to read between the lines and no matter what exhibit empathy, even if you don't understand.

Our words, looks and even actions can simply be that one last push that person does not need before becoming completely broken. We are not here to harm people. We are not even here to fix people. **We are here to give and receive love for each other.** Even in your most frustrated moment, your most aggravated state of mind – if you can demonstrate pure and honest love not just for yourself, but for another human being, then you, my friend, are on the right path.

It'll be a struggle and it'll require a lot of discipline, but it's all we are supposed to do. **Love will exceed all pain, anguish and suffering. Love, understanding and empathy will override anything that person is dealing with.** Share that with the world and leave those battles of the ego on the sidelines.

Today's Daily Affirmation is:

I will keep no record of wrongs.

If we keep a record of everyone's wrongs, we'll never notice when they do something right. You don't want to only see the wrongs a person has done to you or in their life when you look at them. You want to see the love you have for them. If you walked around tallying up everything everyone has ever done to hurt you, betray you, frustrate you, backstab you, etc. – you'll never be able to appreciate or enjoy the good that is taking place every day. **Don't let past hurt steal your joy!**

So if we look for what's right and focus on what's good, the negatives will disappear. Our list of *'rights'* will overshadow the wrongs. My pastor gave a great example – **in sports, you always put the number of your wins above the number of your losses. The number of wins always precedes because those are your accomplishments, and that's what you want others to hear first.** You don't want them to hear all the losses you had – no, those can follow what you've done right! We need to take this and use it in life, relationships and friendships.

Today's Daily Affirmation is:

I stay mindful of my feelings.

The Universe communicates with us through many different ways – animals, objects, people, even television or music. But another crucial way it relays its messages is through our own feelings.

How are you feeling today? What is it that you are feeling about a particular situation? **Listen to yourself. You will not steer you wrong!** It's when we ignore and deny these feelings that we end up along the wrong path. When we accept them, they dissipate, and we can continue receiving the blessings waiting on the other side!

Today's Daily Affirmation is:

I do not dwell on the 'how' or 'when' because I trust divine timing.

Let go of what didn't go right. Stop dwelling on what you didn't get done yesterday or what was supposed to happen. Begin today with a positive spirit. **Have faith that it's all unfolding just as it should – because it is!** Today is going to deliver you all that you've been hoping for if you just let go, stop focusing on the *'how'* and the *'when'* and believe!

Today's Daily Affirmation is:

I will always listen to my soul.

Make time for you daily. **Your soul cannot fulfill its purpose if it is not at peace.** Our daily interactions, the energy we encounter and situations we need to deal with can drain us physically and mentally. This is why it's important to take time for you. If you cannot be at peace alone, you will not be capable of helping anyone else.

Guilt is merely a self-induced mindset. I often hear people say they *'don't have time'* to take for them or *'they feel guilty'*. This has nothing to do with anyone else; this is only their perception and mindset. **You make time for what is important to you, and if guilt is seeping it, that is only negativity trying to block you from pursuing that idea.** *Don't let it win!* Make an intention to give yourself **30 minutes a day of *"me"* time** to do what makes your soul happy. It'll not only increase your intuition; it will enhance your energy, so you can travel through your days with joy, peace, and understanding no matter what comes your way.

Today's Daily Affirmation is:

I fight the negative with the positive.

You don't need to be super intuitive to differentiate between good energy and bad energy. *Have you ever met a person and instantly felt uncomfortable?* Like there's something *'off'* and you can't put your finger on it. That's negative energy. That doesn't mean they're a bad person, it just means they're carrying around an energy that they might not be aware of or have created for themselves.

I encourage you to surround yourself with good energy and people who lift you up instead of drag you down. But I do not encourage you to fight negative energy with negative energy. That means if you get a sip of it when you meet someone or go somewhere, don't feed into it. Energy is powerful and clings to vulnerability – amongst other things. **The best way to fight it is with positive energy. So be you and stand in your power and flood it out with your light and love.**

Today's Daily Affirmation is:

I accept what is in my life.

Acceptance of what is taking place in your life means not complaining about what is happening or what is lacking. Eckhart Tolle says, *"To complain is always non-acceptance of what is."* If you're fighting the process, you're going to be unhappy. If you can go with the flow and just let it all be, willingly, you won't create blocks for yourself, your path or your lessons to happen. **When there are no blocks, you're able to ride the wave of life as it comes with joy, peace, and understanding in your heart and soul.**

Today's Daily Affirmation is:

I do not allow the ego to run my relationships.

A lot of times we think we know what another person is dealing with when really, we don't. That good old saying, *"Don't judge me until you walk a mile in my shoes,"* applies to everyone in life. Every relationship you have needs to be approached with an understanding that even though you may *"think"* you know, you don't. In my job, I practice every day. I may have a gift to be able to empathize and offer guidance and wisdom into someone else's path in life, but I never, ever assume I know them or what they're dealing with.

By judging and assuming, we create a block in a relationship that will get stronger and tougher to break down if we keep at it. But if we're constantly having tension with another person in our life, we need to set aside our ego and approach differently. It doesn't matter if you're younger, older, their boss, or if they're your grandmother – ***ego affects us all equally.**** Until we become self-aware of the ego taking over in our lives, we won't be able to defeat it.

Today's Daily Affirmation is:

I speak goodness into my life.

Our words have power! Speaking poorly of yourself, will affect your life more than you probably ever thought it would. **Speaking negative affirmations about yourself is sending out an energy so strong that the words you speak will be brought into existence.** That's why it's important to watch your words because we all have the power to speak life or death into existence in our lives as well as other's lives.

However, it's a double-edged sword because if you speak poorly of others, that energy will come back around and affect you as well. If you want good things to happen for you and to you, speak love and light into other people's lives. Speak positive affirmations about yourself. *Truly believe them!* With social media these days, it makes this entire idea even more harmful because energy manifests in computers – so what you type works the same as what you think and what you speak out loud! I see far too many people complaining about how horrible they feel their life is and then in the next breath complaining about another person's life and how horrible of a person that individual is and how they don't deserve this, that, or what-have-you. **Perhaps this is why you feel your life is "horrible" – because what we see in others is merely a reflection of what we see in ourselves.**

What other people deserve is none of our business. What they think of us, is none of our business. We are here to give kindness and love and do our part in helping our soul along our own journey. Stop worrying what others are doing. Stop dwelling on what they think or how they perceive you. Don't worry about where you are compared to where they are in life. None of this matters. What matters is how you feel about you – how you perceive you and what you do with your own life path. **Speak goodness into your life.** *Wish well for others. This comes full circle – do it genuinely.* Don't do it selfishly. God knows the difference!

Today's Daily Affirmation is:

I promise to be good to me first.

Spending time alone with yourself is never a bad thing – though many will try to make it seem as if it is. **Getting to know and enjoy your own company is a crucial part of personal and spiritual growth.** If you're aware of who you are and what you like and don't like then, you have already established the important foundation work for your journey. *Once you can trust yourself fully, you'll be less likely to teeter off course on your path.*

Spending time with just yourself does not classify you has a **"hermit"** or **"anti-social"** – *people who throw out these words frivolously do not understand you because they do not understand themselves.* These are probably individuals who constantly need to be surrounded with people because they are unsure of who they are and what they like. Don't get angry with them when they judge you; wish them well, send them peace and continue on your journey. **They are merely obstacles that negativity has sent to distract you and throw you off course.** Remember to always take time for you, every single day – not just once a week, every single day. We all have responsibilities, but one of them that is important is being still with yourself. **Your soul can't grow, and you definitely cannot be good for others if you aren't good to yourself first.**

Today's Daily Affirmation is:

I am aware of the energy I am giving this world.

What do you do when you're surrounded by negative energy? What do you do when you have to interact with someone who doesn't understand the energy they're putting out into the world? **Some people won't, or will refuse to, understand that perhaps they're the one creating the problems in their life and it's not everyone else who they seem to be blaming.**

People aren't always going to be *'on your level.'* You cannot fix people nor can you make them understand something they won't accept or acknowledge. As a life coach, I cannot help everyone – though I'd like to be able to, I also **cannot help people who don't want help.** I might be using myself as an example here, but **everyone's got someone, at least 1 person in their life – perhaps a relative, coworker or maybe even a loved one that blames the world for their problems.** It's always everyone else's fault. *I like to say that when you're pointing the finger at others, there's three more staring right back at you!*

We need to live a life of self-awareness. Being aware of what **YOU** do – your faults, your shortcomings and lessons you need to learn or improve upon. It's quite possibly the hardest thing to do to admit you have something you need to work on – but it's liberating and humbling. **What you put out, you always attract** – so if you seem to be attracting individuals you feel are dramatic, jealous, mean, or needy – take a step back and examine yourself. Is there something in them that you don't like about yourself? Is there something about them you dislike that you should be working on in your own life? There usually is! **Examine yourself today** – I try to find time to do this daily, mostly before bed. **I review my interactions with everyone that day and see what I could improve upon. Not what I could fix for them, what I could fix in me!**

Today's Daily Affirmation is:

I will not speak or think negative about myself.

Have I ever told you how powerful your mind is? It can alter any circumstance just by how you view it. We all go through ups and downs – spells of self-doubt and fear. We wonder if we're doing the right things in our lives or could we be doing more. A lot of times we don't give ourselves enough credit. **We shortchange our unique talents and wisdom and exchange them for self-deprecating thoughts about how we're not good enough, smart enough, pretty enough, successful enough.**

But, what if you exchanged each worrisome thought for a positive affirmation about yourself? Let me tell you how quickly that'll stop the negativity in its tracks: It's like approaching a yellow light on a highway. *The yellow light means slow down – proceed with caution.* **The minute you start thinking something negative about yourself I want you to imagine you're approaching a yellow traffic light.** No one really wants to have to stop, especially when they're rolling down that highway – most people want to make the light and keep going. In order to make that light and not get stopped by the red, which represents your negative thinking – *which will stop you dead in your tracks and keep you there* – you **NEED** to proceed with caution and slow down, **WATCH YOUR THOUGHTS!** You won't be able to move forward if you keep speaking or even thinking negative towards yourself. **Reroute those thoughts when you approach that yellow light and you'll be able to stay on the highway, moving at your speed with nothing but green lights in the distance!**

Today's Daily Affirmation is:

I am uniquely special. I will not compare myself to others.

Be so focused on improving yourself that you don't have time to glance to the side at what others are working towards. Comparing ourselves is a bad habit a lot of us get caught up in. We think we need what they have or we wonder why we're not good enough to have it. What we need to remember is that we all advance along our own paths at our own speeds. My personal growth isn't going to match yours. **It doesn't matter your age or experience – there are things that are uniquely special about you that no one else in this world has to offer.**

Remember this quote the next time you start comparing yourself to someone else: *"A flower does not think of competing with the flower next to it. It just blooms."* **Be your own flower, grow at your own speed and you will blossom when it's your right time to shine! No one can steal your beauty, as each flower is imperfectly perfect in their own way!**

Today's Daily Affirmation is:

When I feel like complaining, I will look for the lesson.

The concept of time is irrelevant when you view it spiritually. Divine timing or God's time is spiritual time. That has nothing to do with minutes, hours, days, weeks, months or years. It's understood in spiritual lessons. Once our spirit has learned a lesson, we move on to the next lesson. Until you **LEARN** certain things, you might not be able to **SEE** all the answers to life's questions.

A basic understanding is that we are spiritual creatures having an Earthly experience – not the other way around. Our bodies are just a shell for our spirit. Our spirit is what is learning, our spirit is what is growing. I would not be where I am or be able to do what I do had I not experienced every single thing I experienced prior to this point in time. **It could not have happened a second sooner because I hadn't learned what I needed to learn along my journey yet.** My physical sight was not always seeing the full picture at times but it wasn't going to until my spirit was on the level it needed to be to **VIEW** the whole picture. My physical mind might have been losing its patience. My physical body might have been frustrated in trying to figure out where I belong and what I am meant to do, **but none of the physical matters when it comes to timing.** Each day we are being taught something new to advance us spiritually.

We easily get frustrated with life, jobs, relationships, money, etc. We think we've experienced it all, and it's **OUR** time to be blessed in these areas of life. Trust me; I've been there! That's the physical talking. But I want you to look at life with your spiritual sight and understand that even when you feel like you've just about had enough – even when you think you've seen or done it all. **EVEN** when you think you can't take any more – be patient. *Easier said than done, right?* **UNDERSTAND** that it's happening for a reason. It's happening to teach you something. It'll keep happening and your blessings will keep getting delayed until you open your eyes to the lesson and accept to learn it.

Today's Daily Affirmation is:

I will not tunnel vision my problems.

The Universe gives you exactly what you need, just when you need it. We all doubt it sometimes – including me. We even question it, but the truth is that we can't always see the bigger picture but God can. ***We're looking at our lives through a telescope, but God's got a bird's eye view!***

When you start having tunnel vision on your problems, you'll have a hard time noticing the synchronistic signs the Universe is delivering you for comfort, peace and wisdom into the truth. Put away the telescope today and open your eyes to the bigger picture.

Today's Daily Affirmation is:

I allow myself to feel.

Pay attention to how you are feeling and then let it go. ***What will be, will be no matter what.*** Feelings help us learn. They teach us about ourselves more profoundly than you could even imagine. They show you your triggers and where the work needs to be done. They also show you what brings you joy and lights you up.

We need to learn to embrace them for what they are – they are an opportunity for us to reflect on ourselves – words, actions and emotions. *Embrace it full force and then let it go.* **Hanging too tightly to any one emotion will not serve you.** That's why in meditation they teach you to be the gentle observer of your thoughts. We assign the meanings to everything in our lives and meanings equal labels. That judgment can hold you back if you let it OR it can move you forward if you allow it. Reflect on this today!

Today's Daily Affirmation is:

I am open to the lessons my relationships offer me.

People are placed in our lives for a reason. I'm sure you've heard this said many times before, but it's a very truthful statement. **Every single person we encounter in our life has a specific purpose – be it to teach us a profound lesson or even a minor one.** To help us, guide us or support us. From our parents to siblings, relatives, friends, enemies and yes, even complete strangers. They all have a divine purpose for you. Whether you get along great or can't find common ground – there's a purpose. **Look for the blessings from these individuals! They are there, they aren't hard to find but you need to learn the lessons they're there to teach!**

Today's Daily Affirmation is:

I allow my inner guidance to direct everything that matters.

When people hurt you, forgive them. When people don't understand you, forgive them. Forgive yourself when you know you've done, said or thought something that wasn't in alignment with your heart. Sometimes people "know not what they do" or say for that matter. Sometimes people just don't get it. Don't blame them, just forgive them. Eventually they will get there, but until then don't get mad, don't hold in anger – let it be. *Your purpose isn't always to take control over a situation – your purpose is to allow your inner guidance to direct everything that matters.* **Be of one mind and let the rest fall into place the way it's supposed to.**

Today's Daily Affirmation is:

Loving myself first is what attracts love into my life.

Your quirks – those little things that probably bug you about yourself, are exactly what make you unique and special. **No two people are alike and embracing your true self is important in really learning how to love you as well as others.** Being able to love yourself, body, personality and individuality provides self-healing inside. **Once you are at peace on the inside, you are able to give and receive love on the outside.** One cannot operate without the other. So if you're struggling in relationships, friendships or even just platonic partnerships – take a look at yourself on the inside. There's probably some tweaking you can do that'll offer a powerful healing only you are capable of providing yourself with.

Today's Daily Affirmation is:

I will stay mindful of every connection I make today.

Be open to the connections the Universe delivers you. **Sometimes we're so busy wanting or even lusting after something else that we miss what's standing in front of us.** People are placed along our paths for a reason – *I've mentioned before how some people are here to help teach us important lessons for our soul to grow*. There are connections being made every single day of your life – from talking to your mailman to the checker at the grocery store. Sometimes it may be brief, but ever so important. Pay attention to each interaction throughout your day – even the ones with animals or children or babies. **Wisdom from above is always being delivered to us and we can only receive it to advance ourselves if we stay mindful of it.**

Today's Daily Affirmation is:

I accept that all external changes start on the inside of me.

Change comes from within. We often confuse it and believe circumstances or people need to change externally and that'll lead to an internal change. This is not right-minded thinking. **If you want your situation to be different, you need to look within yourself.** It could be your perception that needs to change, your attitude or beliefs. You want your relationships to change – look on the inside of you first. *It all starts within!*

If things aren't working so well on the outside…take some time to focus your attention on the inside. Self-growth and improvement are always a positive thing! **It doesn't matter your age or what you've experienced in life, we each should be growing and learning every single day that we're alive and breathing!**

Today's Daily Affirmation is:

When I'm unsure, I release the emotions and step into my calmness.

Sometimes all it takes is to step away from a situation to receive wisdom into it. Spending time with yourself and your thoughts is the only way to learn or be guided on what you should do and how you should do it. **We often allow our emotions and thoughts to overtake us when we're upset, frustrated or confused and when this happens we only think more, get more upset, more frustrated and more confused.**

Be mindful of realizing that when you don't know what to do, do nothing. Take a moment and be with yourself. *Allow your inner guidance to speak to you because it's going to give you insight into what is going on.* **It will not lead you astray.** It'll provide calmness to your situation that you otherwise wouldn't have received through other outlets. The peace and the patience you'll have upon doing this will be undeniable and overwhelming. I promise that you will be filled with so much peace and joy, no matter the situation's context that you won't allow your emotions to ever get the best of you again.

Today's Daily Affirmation is:

I trust that God is always on time with my wants, needs, and desires.

There's always a reason, a divine reason why certain things don't happen for us when WE want them to. *We want what we want when we want it, but God knows better.* God knows we still have things to learn or have to go through some stuff in order to be ready to receive what we're asking for.

That doesn't mean we won't receive it eventually – but we are people of the **"now" mindset.** We want it now, and we always try to find a way to get what we want immediately. If you beg to differ just take a glance at your credit card bill or perhaps your loan payment. Maybe you're debt free, but have you ever driven through a drive-through window to order food? Or perhaps you use an app to order food, track it, book a flight and pick a seat before anyone else – the list goes on and on!

There are plenty of things I thought I was ready for a year ago or two years ago, but looking back now I realize I was far from ready for them. We aren't always able to acknowledge it until time passes and we realize some stuff. I'm speaking generally on purpose here because this doesn't just apply to our careers or relationships – this can apply to anything and everything. Something like a responsibility to be able to do something or a relationship we thought we were ready to have years ago, but we're in a totally different place now. We all progress at different rates as we're all on our own paths and journeys. **Trust that God will keep giving you directions and not steer you wrong and believe and have faith that what you WANT will eventually happen for you** – maybe not in the way you envisioned it or at the time you thought you needed it – but it **WILL** *happen at the right time when you're ready to handle it!*

Today's Daily Affirmation is:

I am grateful for what I receive and don't receive.

You cannot get down on yourself or your life when something doesn't go your way. Take it as a blessing and be grateful. **The Universe is aware of so much more than our minds want to acknowledge.**

Just always remember that your wants, needs and desires will always be fulfilled – maybe not exactly how you expect them to, but what's meant to happen in your life will always have your best interest at hand.

Today's Daily Affirmation is:

I trust myself.

Trust yourself! There are things you are going to know, things you are going to sense and feel that you may never be able to explain – but you do **NEED** to trust them! Regardless of anyone else's abilities, **you know yourself better than anyone else does.** You know what is best for you and what is not! Trust yourself in your decision-making. Trust your intuition – that gut feeling you have! No one knows what your heart desires except for you and the Universe. **Believe in you first, and let everything else fall into place naturally.**

Today's Daily Affirmation is:

I release my worries and let whatever will be, be.

The worries of life can easily consume us. We get worried, frustrated and impatient about thoughts we create in our minds. **Remember though that those worrying thoughts can be brought into existence if you focus on them enough.**

Why not quit the worrying though for good? Why not just let what will be, be? Easier said than done, isn't it? I know, I get it – I've been there. **Let me tell you how God/the Universe works though; when it's TIME** (*not our time, God's time*) **for something to happen, it's going to happen no matter what.** If it's **TIME** for us to learn a lesson, he's going to teach us. How, when and why do not matter – you'll understand those after the fact. If it's **TIME** for our soul to meet someone, we will. It doesn't matter where we are or what we're doing. *Crazy concept, right?*

Relinquish that control that you THINK you have and your heart won't be so heavy with these self-made burdens. Give up the idea that your time is even comparable to God's time. Divine timing is not conventional time. It's not 60 seconds equals 1 minute. *Divine timing is based on our soul's growth.* I've stated this before – we need to go through things, learn things, experience things in order to advance. You can create the thought that you're ready for your one true love, your soulmate to come into your life right **NOW**, but there are things you don't comprehend or even realize. There are things **YOU** must learn if it's not happening yet. All you can do is **TRUST** in divine timing, let go of your fears and let whatever's going to happen, happen.

Today's Daily Affirmation is:

I change my perception to learn my spiritual lessons.

Whenever a situation arises that is creating you pain and angst, it's because you're not perceiving it properly. **Your perception isn't large enough to see the bigger picture. It's so narrow that you're not seeing the GOOD that can come from the situation.** *How many times have you encountered someone who had dealt with a serious physical illness but remained positive about it?* That's because their perception is on point. Now I'm not saying that having a serious illness is a good thing, but those who have to deal with situations like that usually have a better outlook then those who don't and there's a reason for it. *Remember how I always say there's a lesson in every single encounter in our lives?* **Perception = recognizing the lesson!** *If you can't find the lesson in it, change your perception.* Not only will your soul fill with happiness and peace; situations (*no matter what*) will always seem to just flow more smoothly from then on out. Trust me on this!

Today's Daily Affirmation is:

I am not fearful of the truth.

You are often going to encounter people who would rather be told false truths. **They want to hear what will make them feel good instead of what will make them grow.** You could easily hold your tongue to avoid confrontation but you won't be helping anyone by doing that.

Speaking the truth makes you brave. It means you are strong enough to handle it yourself and handle whatever becomes of speaking it. **The truth makes you feel, confront, fix and heal.** Knowing it, speaking it and living it is crucial to your soul's growth. **You are helping other people along their journey by sharing it with them and you're increasing your own vibrations by living a truthful, honest and authentic life.**

By not doing this, you block yourself and decrease your vibrations. It's like taking 10 steps forward and 11 steps back. The truth doesn't have to be given viciously though – dish it out kindly. There's a difference between your *"opinion"* on the matter and the *"truth"* of the matter. Remember this and search within to differentiate. Don't be fearful of the truth – embrace it with all that you are.

Today's Daily Affirmation is:

I am here to learn, grow, and improve who I am. I am here to live my truth.

Some people find it easier not to tell the truth. That's because the truth requires getting really honest with yourself. Being honest with yourself is a courageous act. It requires you to look at your sh*t and own it. But acknowledging areas of personal growth requires openness to actually bettering them. **Personal and spiritual development is the vase of water that feeds the flowers and allows them to grow. If you don't keep the vase full of clean water, the flowers wilt.**

To keep your vase clean, you need to be open and willing to learning more about yourself. *No one is perfect, and no one will ever be perfect.* But we can strive to be kind, caring, honest, loving, truthful, authentic individuals. **We can aim to be the best versions of ourselves we can be!** *Why would you ever want to be anything less?* Teachers aren't perfect, coaches aren't perfect, gurus aren't perfect – but they're all willing to improve every single day.

If you can't face your truth, you are doing your spirit a disservice. It is on Earth to grow, heal and advance. *If you cannot be honest with yourself, how can you be honest with others?* Embrace your journey. Embrace the good, the bad and the ugly. Embrace your mistakes, defeats and your successes. **Embrace ALL of you.** Tell yourself the truth about who you are, how you've grown and where you desire to go in life. **Get real with yourself and know that this life is only here to help you heal any part of you that you haven't fully learned to love yet.** That's what being real and true does.

Today's Daily Affirmation is:

I am exactly where I'm supposed to be.

Just because you don't see things happening the way you'd hope they'd happen doesn't mean they're not going in the direction you want. *God works in mysterious ways.* Where you are right now is where you are meant to be. The route you're taking to get to where you **WANT** to be just might be a different route. **Trust that there are no coincidences and no mistakes.** Everything is as it should be and everything will unfold as it's meant to be. Sometimes we just need a reminder of that!

Today's Daily Affirmation is:

I love and embrace who I am.

Don't alter your mission, your personality, attitude or character to satisfy someone else's judgment. **Your purpose isn't to please everyone; it's to fill your spirit with what brings you joy.** *Too often we listen to the harsh critics of the world instead of our inner voice.* Far too many times we don't stay true to ourselves for fear of what someone else might think or say. You can't live your life this way.

You can't ignore who you are to make others temporarily happy – because their happiness should not be relying on how you act anyhow. They should be looking within as well. **If they're criticizing you, that's a reflection of them and something they need to focus on.** Never place yourself on the back-burner to please the world's critics. You're never going to please them and you aren't meant to!

Today's Daily Affirmation is:

I turn my painful situation into personal growth.

If something upsets us by not going the way we hoped it would go, we need to change our perception of it. **Situations happen to teach us, not harm us.** That doesn't mean we need to be *'okay'* with every bad situation that occurs in our life, but it does mean we need to pay attention to our feelings when something invokes a sudden emotion.

Being mindful in a moment of pain can lead you to a breakthrough. Practicing this daily can help you grow and provide you so much wisdom into life and into your own personal journey. Now this doesn't mean we'll be able to avoid pain all-together but it does mean that we'll learn **FROM** it more easily, instead of letting our ego take over with thoughts like *"I don't deserve this,"* *"why does this always happen to me,"* *"my life sucks."*

Today's Daily Affirmation is:

I focus my energy on only the good things I want in my life.

Focus on the things you do want, rather than focusing on all the things you don't want in your life. This is really important because what we put our energy into, we manifest into reality. If you're dwelling on the bad, you're manifesting more of it. If you keep your eye on the good or the things you **WANT** to happen, you're lifting your vibrations which will manifest your wants into reality.

Today's Daily Affirmation is:

I am not afraid to share my feelings.

Communication is a vital part of relationships and if we don't know how to share, then we don't know how the other is feeling. If we don't know how the other is feeling, we make assumptions created from our own minds about how the person is feeling. This only leads to trouble.

If you don't know, ask! If you feel something, share! Simple yet so hard for so many to do. **Staying mindful of our feelings and sharing them with our partner is the only way for two people to live a life as one.** Just as they teach you in any sport to talk to your teammates, call for the ball if you got it or shout if you're open so they can pass to you – this integrates perfectly into all types of relationships we're going to encounter along our journey. Whether it's love, lust or friendship – you need to practice communication.

Today's Daily Affirmation is:

I am mindful of the energy I give this world.

Give this world good energy! We wake up with a choice and that choice is solely up to you. What you put out into this world will always, **ALWAYS** be returned to you tenfold. This doesn't always happen immediately, though sometimes it does. The point is that you are responsible for your own energy and it's very important you keep it positive.

If you put out negative energy, you'll receive it in return. So if things aren't going your way, *flip it and reverse it* – try doing something nice unexpectedly for someone and watch what happens in your own life. Try holding the door for a stranger or smiling and waving hi! **These may seem like small gestures, but it's the energy and intent that is behind them that is powerful.** If you're just going through the motions, the Universe knows. So make it genuine and be mindful of it always!

Today's Daily Affirmation is:

I am grateful for all that I have in this present moment.

Pause for a minute today and take it all in. See the things you already have going on in your life – the people, the 'stuff', the love – *now give the Universe a giant Thank-You!* **Often we're too busy looking at what is missing from our lives that we fail to actually notice what's already in our lives.** When I catch myself doing this, I too need to pause and look around and show some gratitude. We always want the things we can't have. Too many times we fail to appreciate the things we do have until we lose them. Let's change all that shall we and start really showing gratitude for what is already in our life. **There once was a time we had hoped we'd have what we have now and you see how easily that is forgotten.**

Today's Daily Affirmation is:

I step out of my comfort zone with peace, strength, and confidence.

When we step out of our comfort zones, even for a brief second, amazing things happen. It's funny how the mind can work for you and against you – all at the same time – especially when we have an opportunity to step out of our comfort zones. The mind wants to stop you and say no while that inner voice is saying yes.

Always listen to that inner voice telling you yes – that's the voice that's going to get you to your breakthrough. If you keep listening to your mind finding reasons for you to say no, you'll always be stuck in the same situation because you'll never venture outside the box.

Today's Daily Affirmation is:

I trust that whatever happens is always meant in my best interest.

You cannot force an outcome. You cannot make something happen that isn't meant to happen. We all struggle with this in different ways during our life – be it in our jobs, families or even relationships. *Forcing something creates an energy that'll block your desired outcome.* This stems from fear, stubbornness and not practicing patience. I learned this the hard way many times. **You need to trust that what will be, will be – no matter what the outcome is, it's the one that is in your best interest.** Once you can truly grasp this, it becomes easier to release and let go of wanting to be in control.

Today's Daily Affirmation is:

When I feel like my patience has run out, I silence my ego and remain calm.

Patience. Something we often overlook and take for granted. **Good things come to those who wait and just when you think you've waited long enough, my advice to you is to keep waiting.** God has a plan for you – a very specific, well-thought out plan. He has your best interest at heart and will not lead you in the wrong direction.

When we think we know better, we have let our ego speak louder than our inner guidance. When we think we've been patient long enough, that's our ego doing the talking. That ego can be a trouble-maker and delay your blessings if you listen to it too often. *Silence the ego and understand that when the time is right, it'll happen.*

Today's Daily Affirmation is:

I am present, grateful, and calm when life tries to overwhelm me.

Sometimes we get so caught up in the day-to-day that we become overwhelmed and lose sight of what's important. We often let worries and concerns, fears, dreams and even hopes cloud our vision. Don't misunderstand me, it's completely okay, more than okay to hope and dream – but today's reminder is to *stay present*. I was traveling recently and hadn't done so in quite some time. It's easy to think you'll be able to take a quick trip, return and get right back into your routine.

It isn't always that easy...but here's how you can let it be: **Remember that everything will get done when it should. Remember to listen to your body and your intuition. Remind yourself that the important things are to breathe, remain calm, be kind and have gratitude for all that you have and all that you are.** *The rest will take care of itself if you take care of yourself first.*

Today's Daily Affirmation is:

I am in control of creating my life by maintaining control over my thoughts.

Life is comprised of situations we create for ourselves. Let me explain – if you think about something enough, eventually – energetically it's going to manifest into your reality. Good or bad things. So when you get mad at your circumstances, you need to stop pointing the finger at everyone else and look within yourself.

It's not an easy task to take responsibility for situations we aren't too happy about. But this is the way energy works. **This is how negative energy wins – it makes you believe the bad in all things. It blinds you from the good. It clouds the truth.** When you feed into it, you give it more power over you and your life. When you dismiss it, it loses strength.

Yes, it's that simple. But the mind is such a complex creature that works simplistically; we often get confused. We struggle, doubt and question. We aren't able to grasp how a simple switch in perception can alter an entire reality – but it can. It still can, no matter what you have happening in your life right now, it can. Change your perception.

Today's Daily Affirmation is:

I am kind, forgiving, and do not engage when approached with hate.

Let's talk about hate. I don't like using the word hate which is quite funny because growing up and not knowing any better I remember using it very often for the most pointless things from, *"I hate wearing a snowsuit"* to *"I hate waking up early."* I clearly didn't know any better as most children use this word often. Thankfully I've grown and evolved a lot since then, and I have eliminated that word from my vocabulary.

Let's keep it brief– people feel as if they are entitled to say whatever they want from behind a computer screen. Little do they realize their words *(yes, even written)* have just as much power as they do when thought or spoken. **Hateful words over social media are common these days, and even I encounter them when people comment on my articles on the website or other social media pages. Not everyone is going to love you. Not everyone is even going to like you. They're not all going to like what you do, how you talk, how you dress, your beliefs or anything about you for that matter. Don't make this your problem. Do not take on the burden that should remain theirs.**

There is something about you that is trying to teach their soul a lesson *(whether you know or speak to these people or not)* and they're ego is fighting it with hate because it doesn't want to grow and learn. Your light is bright and their darkness is reacting to it. **There is something about you they want, need or see in themselves that they've abandoned or judged.** You don't need to engage with their fear though because you cannot help them heal it – you are only there to poke it to the surface. You don't need to do anything but be kind and move forward. **Gabby Bernstein** says, *"forgive and delete."*

Today's Daily Affirmation is:

I stay centered and grounded when chaotic energy tries to lead me off course.

Find the things that bring you peace and always return to them when you feel as if it is straying from you. I, too often forget when I get stressed or begin to lose my cool that the answer is simple – go back to the basics, *return to what keeps me grounded and balanced.* **Stressful energy is chaotic energy, and its purpose is to lead you off course.** The way we defeat it is by staying centered in our truth.

Today's Daily Affirmation is:

I am mindful and open to receive the guidance and wisdom I need.

Pay attention! You are consistently receiving divine hints and guidance daily, but you need to pay attention. If you have too much pride to listen or can't let go of your stubbornness, you will miss them. They come as strangers, messages, random songs or even the *'irony'* of a television show.

People could be walking right up to you and giving you the message *(without knowing it)* **and if your eyes and ears are shut, you'll never see or hear the wisdom.** Open your eyes, unclog your ears and start paying attention and being mindful of everything you encounter in the present moment. **All the questions you have, any confusion you're going through – the comfort and advice you are seeking is staring you right in the face.**

Today's Daily Affirmation is:

I am supportive and loving in my thoughts about myself.

We can be our own worst enemies OR we can be our own best friends? It's really your choice which you choose to be. I'm really hard on myself – harder than anyone else has or will ever be on me. That's my nature and I know that about myself so being aware of it I know I have to give myself extra love and care. I need to keep the words I say and think about myself positive. **But if you are hard on yourself and you allow your self-talk to become negative and self-deprecating then that's when you become your own worst enemy.** *Remind yourself that it all starts with you – your words, your thoughts, your actions – so if you don't believe in you, no one will.*

Today's Daily Affirmation is:

I am present.

To be present is one of the most important things we need to be doing while we're here and alive. When our mind is elsewhere and we're not focused on the here and now, we miss so much.

I'm not talking about surface experiences – *I'm talking about depth, spiritual wisdom, and soulful lessons.* **We can only be open enough to learn if we are present.** The mind easily wanders, but to remain present is a discipline. It's an art they don't teach us in school – it's something you learn from what I like to call *"on-the-job experience"*. **That's how you learn some of the best stuff – by practicing it daily and putting it into motion.** Not someone telling you how, not reading why out of a book – just doing it.

Use your gifts that you were born with – those being your peace, patience and your open spirit. Because the opposites of those are self-created (mis-created, *mind you*) here on Earth. **Our spirits are so mindful and willing – so open and honest – so loving and patient that you'd be surprised how easy everything flows when you release those mis-creations and your ego and you stay present and just take everything in.**

Today's Daily Affirmation is:

I am capable of anything.

Hard-work pays off. When you set an intention to accomplish something, nothing can hold you back if you're determined and have willpower. Don't underestimate the power of an intention. If you set your mind to the right channel, anything is possible.

When people say *something* that you have an intention of accomplishing is impossible, don't let that sway you. That is them projecting their doubts, worries and fears onto you. That is their negative energy working through them to hold you back. "That is them assigning their lack of belief in themselves doing it to you." They can have their fears and concerns, but you don't need to accept them, acknowledge them **OR** take them on as your own. Be strong, stay focused and above all else trust yourself. **You are capable of anything that brews from your heart – believe it!**

Today's Daily Affirmation is:

I am my truth.

Don't fear your truth. Don't worry about what so-and-so thinks of your path in life. Don't get frustrated when people don't support your journey. You are beautifully and wonderfully made, and you have such unique gifts to offer this world.

Sure a lot of us, especially in the field I work in are re-purposing the same content – but the way I coach may resonate with someone differently than the way another person coaches. The way I coach is based off of my perception of what I've learned and that perception comes from my life experiences. **Since all our life experiences are different, the way we all perceive the same things is going to be different.** So don't compare, don't judge and don't ever think that because someone doesn't understand you, you're doing something wrong. Follow your path and always, always, always trust yourself.

Today's Daily Affirmation is:

I am grateful.

Gratitude – a word we hear a lot but do we have an understanding of what it is? Gratitude is not only a readiness to show appreciation for something but it's also a readiness to return the kindness. You see you can read or hear someone say they are grateful (*feeling or showing thanks) for their life/boyfriend/family/job/friends/dog/etc. – but are they just words or are they actually **SHOWING** the appreciation?

Let me put it to you this way – the first thing you usually do upon receiving a gift from someone else is say, *"Thank You."* Most times you follow that thank you with a hug or a kiss or for some, another kind favor in return. *So what do you do/say/think when you open your eyes each morning and see daylight?* Mumble and grumble, struggle to get out of bed and get ready for work **OR** do you wait a second, *realize this day was gifted to you and* **SHOW** *gratitude for that gift by spreading kindness wherever you go?*

Okay, so sure – reading the above might sound super fluffy, I understand that (I handle the cynics of the world daily) **HOWEVER, today I challenge you to try it. SHOW gratitude for something like the fact that you even woke up** *(because some people didn't!)* **and just watch what happens!** *Gratitude is ALWAYS returned in some way, shape or form.*

Today's Daily Affirmation is:

I am powerful and capable of anything I choose to focus on.

Step into your own power. All during my meditations lately, I have been receiving a very similar message and that was, "**You are more powerful than you think.**" *Sometimes we doubt that though, don't we?* Sometimes we scoff at ourselves and think, *"impossible!"*

We are very unfair to ourselves because all power starts within. Only when you question and doubt do you diminish your own power. Today I want you to put an end to that completely! *YES…COMPLETELY!* **Stop doubting yourself, your talents, abilities, wisdom and truth. Stop belittling yourself for the things you think you are not.**

You are everything you think about yourself – the good and the bad. For some reason we have an easier time believing the bad over the good. *FLIP IT* as I always say – toss out the bad and remind yourself you are powerful and capable of anything.

Today's Daily Affirmation is:

I am enough.

You are not the victim. You are so strong on the inside! Don't allow your ego to let you think for one second that this is not so. **You are more than capable and you are enough. The power is within you.** Trust that it's there because it is. **You just need to acknowledge it to access it.**

Today's Daily Affirmation is:

I am willing to receive.

Be at peace with who you are becoming. Understand your strengths and your weaknesses and where you need to grow. **Improvement is not a negative word.** It's something you should always be striving for. Some of us think that if we confess or admit at least to ourselves that we need to *"improve"* upon something then we've failed. This is not so – there is always something to learn and always something you can grow from. Sometimes we'll learn from ourselves – other times it could be from an unsuspecting source. **Keep your eyes, ears and your heart wide open and willing to receive the lessons that are out there waiting for you.**

Today's Daily Affirmation is:

I am mindful of each and every moment that happens today.

Everything begins somewhere. **If life was meant to flash by without lessons and connections, then it would.** But here's the truth – **each day we wake up we're meant to experience fully with our eyes wide open.** The people we pass or speak to and connect with – they've been sent to us that day for a purpose. The things we end up doing whether planned or unplanned – they were meant to take place. **Every single thing has its place and purpose.** It begins somewhere, and if you're mindful of each day, you'll soon realize it comes around full circle.

Recently something I experienced when I was younger came around full circle and it ended up explaining to me some of the things I'm doing right now in my life. I challenge you to open your eyes and pay attention to everything during your days. **Everything will begin to make sense as you become more mindful of each moment.**

Today's Daily Affirmation is:

I am important.

Never feel guilty for looking after yourself. **Taking care of yourself and finding time for you is crucial to your soul.** I'm sure these words have been written by me before but **you can't help anyone if you're not helping yourself first.** I have to remind myself of this often because of what I do for a living. I need to constantly set intentions to take moments just for myself, which I won't lie, isn't always easy. Sometimes you create guilt when you try to take *"me-time"* and sometimes you just feel like there are more important things to be doing. You want to please and accommodate others, but it's most important to please and accommodate yourself first otherwise you're trying to give to others on empty when truly if you were to fill up first...giving becomes an extension of yourself.

Today's Daily Affirmation is:

I am real.

You are never going to be able to please everyone you ever encounter so the most important thing for you to focus on is being yourself. **Stay true to you. Be real and authentic with every encounter and every endeavor.** The people that are meant to be in your life will always be there.

You see what happens when you're not being true to who you are; you try to mold yourself into what *"they"* are or what you think they want or like. *When that happens we end up having relationships or friendships with individuals that aren't meant to last.* **If you show the truly authentic you that your spirit wants you to share with this world, the right people will flock to your side.**

Today's Daily Affirmation is:

I am present and free.

It's really quite hard to master but it's important that we stay present in our lives all the while allowing ourselves to be free. Free from fear. Free from worry. Free from doubts. Free to receive. Free to accept. Free to believe. Being free means not allowing your mind to future-trip or wander. Stay mindful of the present moment and release everything else to the Universe.

Today's Daily Affirmation is:

I release my anger and welcome a blessing instead.

We all have those days where every single thing seems to annoy us. We get upset or bothered by what people say or do, and we really don't know why. I'm not about to try to explain why this happens because quite frankly I don't know. But what I do know is that if you allow the anger to get the best of you. **If you allow it to overtake you and run your day, you're going to miss a whole lot of good stuff.**

So instead of feeding into the negativity today, turn your anger into a blessing because if you feed the fears and the anger and frustration…energetically you WILL create more of it. However, if you feed the positive stuff that you desire to feel, see, and experience, you'll create more of that too. It's equal. When something is about to upset you or you find yourself annoyed for no reason – search for some gratitude in that situation. **When you can find the gratitude, you often find the lesson. When you can find the lesson, you often find the blessing!**

Today's Daily Affirmation is:

I am the answer.

Often we overlook things staring us right in the face. *At times we think searching will reveal something we didn't know or allow us to find something we didn't have.* This isn't the case. **You already have all the answers inside of you.** You already know the answer to that question you're pondering. You already know the next move to make without asking how to make it.

You already know. Stop searching. **The answers to your life are not out on the freeway. You don't even need to pull out of your driveway to find them.** Nope, they are all within you. Don't worry because if you're unsure of it, you'll be given a clear sign of it!

Today's Daily Affirmation is:

I am taking it as it comes.

Take it as it comes. You can't predict the outcome but no matter what it'll have your best interest at hand. Your journey is not meant to hurt you, harm you or discourage you. That's what the Devil wants you to believe. **Your journey is a test.** It teaches you lessons. It's there to help you grow and learn so you can be ready for what's waiting for you. If we aren't willing to grow and learn then what's waiting for us won't be as amazing as it's meant to be.

Today's Daily Affirmation is:

I am peace in the midst of chaos.

No matter how organized, structured and balanced you think you are – life just has a silly little way of tossing out curve-balls when you least expect them. I constantly go through hills and valleys of staying focused, organized and feeling balanced. We are only human and we can't expect to keep it all together all the time – *no matter how hard we try.*

It's easy to get frustrated when this happens because no one likes being thrown off-kilter – not even me. When you go through bouts of feeling overwhelmed, under-appreciated, stressed or just worn out – **take it in stride.** *Let yourself feel these emotions.* Stress management isn't about never having stress because that's impossible. **The goal is to have a mindset that despite the stressful situations, you can still find peace within.** You can teach yourself to understand that it's all happening for a reason. **God wants you to slow down right now. He purposely made you over-sleep or get stuck in traffic. Don't point the finger at others and don't blame yourself for things like this. You can't control the way the Universe works. You just need to accept it for what is it.**

There's no reason to misinterpret the emotions, just feel them and be at peace with them. **People don't always understand my calmness – that I can be at peace no matter what is happening around me.** *It's the simple concept of accepting that you are not in control. Trusting God and the Universe to take care of you always and looking for the lessons in what you experience.* Trust me, it has taken years of self-care, self-love, self-discipline and truly getting to know my spirit, my soul and myself to reach this place of peace that for so long I admired in a mentor of mine. It all starts with you though and you too can reach this place of inner peace that is the root that holds all the branches of your life together.

Today's Daily Affirmation is:

I attract what I feel I am.

Your worth is more than what someone else says it is. Your worth is based on how you feel about yourself. It has nothing to do with the amount of money you make, the way you dress or who your friends are. However, how you feel about yourself will attract these types of things into your life. **If you don't think you're worthy of being around good people, you won't be.** If you don't feel you are worthy of earning a certain amount of money – as if you don't deserve it – you're placing up a barrier between you and a blessing that you deserve.

Sometimes we think we're confident in ourselves, and then life tosses us one of those curve-balls we love so much which makes us realize we probably weren't as grounded in that feeling as we thought we were. **I challenge you to look at yourself. Take notice of your interactions. What makes you smile, what upsets you and what makes you tick. There's knowledge in there for you.** This knowledge helps you understand yourself better. **When you can understand yourself, you will learn to love yourself. Once you can reach that point, you will see how the Universe works in your favor attracting what you desire in your direction!**

Today's Daily Affirmation is:

I am in the moment.

Little by little everything begins to make sense in our lives. You don't even need to believe that sentence when you read it – ***just be patient and watch the synchronous events unfold.*** You'll get this major light-bulb, "AH HA!" moment where things just begin to make sense. **So if you're doubting or worrying that your life is out of order, don't! Don't doubt at all – life is happening for us not to us and we just need to ride the wave as it comes, trust and enjoy it all!**

Today's Daily Affirmation is:

I own my own blessings.

Pay no mind to those trying to tear you down. **They see something in you they wish they had. Problem is that they'll never get what you have because it is divinely yours.** Your gifts and blessings, your spirit and soul – they belong to you and only you. Don't allow those who crave what you have make you think they'll get it. They have their own blessings specifically made for them if they'd focus their attention on who they are, rather than who you are. Keep pursuing your life purpose and filling your spirit with what makes it happy and let them get caught up in your wake of success. Until they realize they can pave their own path, they'll continue to trail behind yours.

Today's Daily Affirmation is:

I am letting go of it all and enjoying where it takes me.

It's a good time to stop worrying and just go with the flow. You can't control any outcome no matter how hard you try. You can't control what is meant to happen. Just let it go, let it all go. The fear, the worry, the anxiety – release it and stay present in the moments. **These moments won't repeat themselves. They're precious and should be treated as such.** So keep your mind where your body is, strap yourself in and enjoy the ride. *Nothing is meant to harm you. Your best interest is always at hand. Have a little faith and just go with it.*

Today's Daily Affirmation is:

I am on the right path.

Life is lived forward but only understood backwards. *It is only when we've lived through something that we can really understand why it took place.* But don't ever get so caught up in reflecting that you miss the here and now. *Why mess up today worrying about tomorrow? Why spoil today worrying about yesterday?* **We can be troubled by what we do know and by what we don't know regardless but the truth of the matter is the road you're on in your life at this very moment –** *you chose it.* **It's part of your curriculum. It's your own unique path.** The lessons on it are there specifically for you. Sure you'll probably comprehend everything and piece it all together better after the fact, so a little reflection is positive. **But don't look behind you too long because the good stuff is all ahead.**

Today's Daily Affirmation is:

I am getting what I need at all times.

We don't always get what we want, but we do always get what we need. The good news is that usually by the time you receive it, you realize you want it. You realize that it far surpasses what you **THOUGHT** you had wanted. *So when you find yourself dwelling and doubting – losing your patience for something or someone just take a deep breath and realize the Universe has your back.* **You won't be given anything before you're ready for it because you'll never fully appreciate all it has to bring you.** Divine timing is everything and it never screws up!

Today's Daily Affirmation is:

I embrace adversity with a strong mind and open heart.

Don't let adversity lead you astray. Allow it to teach you. Be open to learning from it. Don't let it get the best of you or drag you down into a spiral of negativity. Resistance, pressure, stress – use it to your advantage. *Contrast is how we learn.* It delivers the wisdom but you often don't realize that till after it passes! **It's not easy to overcome but if you're mindful of it you can access the strength and power to rise above and learn from it.**

Today's Daily Affirmation is:

I am listening, not just hearing.

When we resist or ignore, we're still going to have to confront what we're trying to avoid. **If you ignore the signs, that isn't going to make them simply disappear.** Embrace what comes your way. What you're avoiding is often what you need to do/say/feel/hear the most!

Listen; don't just hear what people are telling you. Address what it is you need to address. **God uses people in your life. He works through them to help you.** If you refuse to listen, he will find a way to make you listen.

Today's Daily Affirmation is:

My life is uniquely mine and no one can take that from me.

Your experiences, your stories, your path are unique to you. No one can take them from you. They're yours to share and yours to remember. They taught you individual lessons to help you grow. The common theme here is *'you'*. I want you to remember that people may try to imitate, people may try to copy and people may want so badly to have what you have. But don't let that upset you. Don't let it deter you, frustrate or even anger you. **This is your life and you're the lead role. They can star in it, co-star, or even be an extra, but it's individually yours.** It belongs to you and no one can take that from you.

Today's Daily Affirmation is:

I am not comparing myself to anyone. I have my own special blessings with my name on it.

Do you know how much of yourself you take for granted and diminish when you start comparing yourself to other people? Comparing looks, friends, lifestyles, jobs, relationships – this all dims your individual sparkle. You are literally putting energy into the world that you wish you were someone else. That you wish you had someone else's blessings, yet these blessings do not belong to you. While you keep trying to create your life through others, they're busy pleasing their own spirits. **Why are you depriving your own? Why aren't you feeding it what it needs? It doesn't need what others have. It needs you to start watering your own grass instead of admiring your neighbors.**

Today's Daily Affirmation is:

I am vibing with this thing called life.

Stay present today. Live in the moment. **Pay attention to what's happening for you, to you and around you.** Immerse yourself in the experience called life. **These moments won't repeat themselves. These moments are precious. They are teaching you.** Life is one big fun classroom. Enjoy it. Embrace it. Learn from it. Laugh at it. Keep your mind in it today and don't let it wander outside of each present moment. **Free yourself from future-tripping and just vibe with what comes your way right now.**

Today's Daily Affirmation is:

I am believing I will receive what I have asked the Universe for in due time.

The saying goes, *'ask, believe and receive.'* None of these work without the other. **You can't ask and just receive because believing is the glue that holds this threesome together!**

You must believe that you will in fact receive what it is you have prayed for...asked the Universe for. You can't doubt, dwell or question when, how, or how long. Be patient in knowing that you have been heard and when the time is right you will receive what is in your best interest. **It may not be how you expected it. It may not be exactly when you wanted it – but it will come in due time (which is the perfect divine time).** Trust and believe.

Today's Daily Affirmation is:

I am accepting my blessings and not questioning them.

It's easy to fall back into old habits. It's comfortable at times when you search for something you are used to, familiar with. *But it's not always good to do this because as they say, if it's in the past it should stay there right?* Yes, absolutely right. **Don't punish people in your life now for what others in the past have done to you.** It's definitely easier said than done, but it must be done.

God opens new doors for us whether we think we are ready or not and then the Devil will work overtime to close those doors or make us doubt those new connections. **God wouldn't open that door for you unless he felt you were ready for it.** Unless you were prepared and well-equipped for what it had in store for you…otherwise he wouldn't have given it to you.

This could be in your career, spiritual path or in your friendships or relationships. When you think you're ready, you may not truly be ready. **But divine timing is everything and God could give it to you when you least expect it, just when you give up on it or forget about it and you need to take it as it comes!** Things I felt I was ready for 2 years ago, I now realize I had a lot more that I needed to go through, experience and prepare for. But if God brought it to you, it's yours, take it! *Don't doubt the gift God blessed you with. Don't question it.* **Take it and trust that you will be guided, advised, directed and given the wisdom to appreciate it the way you should!**

Today's Daily Affirmation is:

I am allowing what's meant for me to come my way however it sees fit.

We fail to realize that our reality is merely our own perception of what is. Clients often hear me say **"change your perception," "alter your perspective,"** yet these are a lot easier said than done at times. That's why I encourage viewing life through your spiritual eyes. **Accepting what is but understanding there's more under the surface. Enjoying what comes but realizing the depth of it.** This kind of living allows you to maintain an inner peace and acceptance. It helps you release control to a higher power and let what's meant for you come your way at the right time.

Today's Daily Affirmation is:

I am grateful for all the beauty the Universe brings my way.

When you think the worst, you block your perception from seeing the best. You also put out a negative energy and will draw in other negative factors, circumstances and people. The saying goes that when you look for something, you will find it. **So if you're looking for something to be wrong, you are putting that energy out there, manifesting it into reality.** This is a difficult one to overcome at times, as I struggle personally with this as well. The trick is to instantly stop yourself and look for the good.

Gratitude is an amazing way to prevent yourself from manifesting negativity into your life. Flip that feeling and reverse it with something you're grateful for. I challenge you today to list out 3 or more things that are in your life right now that bring you joy. When you list out the good in your life, the bad or what we perceive as bad fades away. You will be amazed at how this increases your energetic vibrations and attracts more beauty into your life.

Today's Daily Affirmation is:

I am releasing, allowing, and accepting what is.

Let go and just allow. When we try to control and manipulate situations and their outcomes, we just receive resistance. **Typically, the outcome never goes the way we had hoped when we try to make something happen rather than just allowing it to happen.** It's a lot easier said than done to just allow things to happen rather than control them happening. *Thing is, when we just release, allow and accept – we receive exactly what we **NEED**!* Focus on this. **Rather than assuming or controlling – accept what is, release what you thought and just allow that situation or person to be authentic to you.** This is how miracles unfold!

Today's Daily Affirmation is:

I am allowing it to flow to me, with me, and for me.

Breathe! Everything is going to be okay. Everything is happening just as it should, the way it should and at the right time it should. You have no reason to ever panic. The Universe has your back. You are being watched over and taken care of. **Your best interest is always at hand and you can trust that when it's time for you to move in one direction or the next, you will know.** Until then, remain at peace with what is and just allow what's meant for you to come into your life.

Today's Daily Affirmation is:

Mindfulness brings me joy.

Today's affirmation will be crucial in keeping you present and grateful today. **When you are able to be present, fully in the moment that is right now – then you can truly be grateful for everything happening in that moment.** *The minute we allow ourselves to leave the present moment, we lose our joy and our gratitude.*

Today, focus on being mindful of anything and everything happening for you. Yes...FOR you! Small things, large things, people, interactions, encounters, experiences – all of it adds up. All of it provides you with insight into your life and yourself. All of it gives you wisdom. All of it provides you happiness. You will regain your joy no matter what is happening by distracting yourself with gratitude. It's not exactly a distraction though because what it does is flip the mindset – trick the energy – **REPLACE** it with what is. Accepting **AND** allowing what is right now releases your need to fear and control. **When you can release those strongholds, you can be filled back up with joy for what you've been given.**

Today's Daily Affirmation is:

I am trusting myself no matter what.

Trust yourself in all that you do. Trust your feelings and decisions. Trust your life's purpose. We don't always give ourselves enough credit for our own gifts. I sure don't – I'm pretty hard on myself all the time. **But I always come back to that place of realizing that in this world I am doing the best I can with the information I have on hand.** We can't always be so hard on ourselves and we need to stop doubting who we are and what we do. If you don't believe in you, *who else is going to?*

Today's Daily Affirmation is:

I flow to my soul's rhythm.

Find your rhythm. Your days, each moment needs to flow with you – resonate with you, inspire you, motivate you. Everyone's flow is different. What works for me probably won't work for you and vice versa. Use what works and stick to it.

When you maintain a rhythm within your soul, you get sh*t done! **When you keep the focus on what makes you happy and speaks to you internally, you'll find that inspiration will just come to you – you won't have to search for it.**

Today's Daily Affirmation is:

I am grateful for the lessons and the blessings.

Sometimes when things are actually going our way we drive ourselves crazy looking for something bad amongst the good. Self-sabotage is a destructive and unhealthy habit. You unintentionally create a problem because you're expecting something bad to occur. **"Nothing can be THAT good,"** is a prime thought in your brain. **You need to start realizing that God didn't put you here to suffer.** Yes, we experience suffering, but only if you perceive it as that. **You could change your perception and think of it as a lesson for yourself. Perceive it as a way to protect you, advance you or help you grow.**

There is no need to sabotage the good in your life, because no matter what you attempt to do, if it's meant for you it's going to stick around regardless. *So quit playing the fool!* Let the good come your way. Embrace it, enjoy it and be grateful for it.

Today's Daily Affirmation is:

I am listening to my inner guide on full blast.

Don't allow pressure from external sources to sway you from what brews in your heart. Pressure is always going to exist. It's going to come when you don't want it, need it or especially when you least expect it.

When it hits you, stop and breathe! **Refocus on what's within you.** Don't let external factors lead you astray – allow your inner guide to be on the loud speaker and help you stay on your path. **Sometimes when you start taking directions from everyone on the sidelines you get lost, confused and overwhelmed.** Listen to your intuition, don't let the pressure weigh you down – *use it as leverage to build you up!*

Today's Daily Affirmation is:

I am constantly learning, growing, evolving, and changing to be the best version of me there is.

We go through hills and valleys of staying mindful to the happenings around us, and then overlooking them and taking them for granted. I've noticed my ego getting the best of me before, and I was overlooking the small things around me that I should have been appreciating. **I realized that these things I'm taking for granted were things I had been praying for, for a very long time. I realized that instead of constantly looking for tiny things to complain about, I should just be grateful for what is.** I centered myself and brought balance back into my life by acknowledging that I'm not always as mindful as I should. *Admitting and accepting your faults does that!*

Everything could be gone in a second. Before I had it, I wanted it and now that I have it, I'm complaining about it. *No – that shouldn't be.* But I'm not alone in these feelings – many of my clients and others I speak with struggle with the same things. **I think we all as humans struggle with this because as much as we want to try to stay mindful and really be grateful – life happens; sh*t happens.** We lose our cool *(yes, even the most zen people lose their cool at times!)*. **We lose our patience; we forget what's important. This is life. This happens to everyone. No one is perfect.** I can't be a teacher without always being a student. I'm always learning and growing from my own personal lessons and from my interactions with family, friends, clients, strangers, etc. **If I never admitted my struggles, I wouldn't be real. If I never confessed I have moments where I forget my own words of wisdom, I wouldn't be human. The teacher is always the student.** I always repeat this to myself. **My growth helps your growth. Your growth helps my growth. We are all connected, we are all one.** Remember this today!

Today's Daily Affirmation is:

I know better therefore I do better.

Sometimes we get into funks. God puts us into a funk – a mental funk, emotional funk, physical funk to teach us something. To wake us up because we know better. **We know better but the problem is we don't always do better.** We know it in our minds, and yet we do the opposite in our words or actions.

It's time that we know better, and we do better. Now how exactly do we go about doing that? We stop being quick to react. Stop being first to respond. Slow down for a minute. Before you act or speak, *check yourself.* Remember that the wisdom lies within you already. You already **KNOW** what you should be doing – the trick is to just **DO IT** *(Nike wasn't so out there in saying that!).* If you're unsure, listen to your intuition – meditate – be still, just **SHUT UP** quite frankly because you have all you need and often times these **"funks"** we're in, we caused them ourselves. We let our ego take over and you will know when that happens, you will feel completely unbalanced, moody, doubtful, anxious, etc. **Bench that ego before it gets the best of you and know that without the funk you'd never receive the wisdom.**

Today's Daily Affirmation is:

I am proud of who I've become.

No matter what, be proud of yourself! Be proud of who you are and how far you've come. **You've gone through what you went through for a reason, and you are here, right now for a reason.** *Be proud!*

Be proud of your growth, your determination and your perseverance. **Don't forget the lessons you've learned and the obstacles you've overcome. Look back with joy and a calmness in your heart knowing that all those hurdles led you to this moment right now.**

Today's Daily Affirmation is:

I am offering my gifts to the world no matter what.

A message I once heard in church reminded me of a beautiful quote by Mother Teresa, *"If you are kind, people may accuse you of ulterior motives. Be kind anyway. If you are honest, people may cheat you. Be honest anyway..."* Let your light shine bright. Give your gifts to the world. Offer them to the world and let that fill you up with joy.

There will be people who try to stomp out your spark and kill your joy. There will be opposition and people who don't receive your gifts, but you must offer your gifts anyway. Offer them and be happy. ***Be happy because it is not between you and them – it is between you and God.*** So continue to be happy anyway. Continue to shine bright anyway. Continue to give your gifts to the world anyway.

Today's Daily Affirmation is:

I am putting my spark into this world with passion and faith.

When you follow your passion and live your purpose, you put something into this world that wasn't there before. You are as individually unique as a fingerprint. *You can't be duplicated!* What you have to offer this world is special.

When you lose yourself in self-created confusion and chaos, you dull your sparkle. **Remind yourself today just how amazing you are. Remind yourself that fear is an illusion. Remind yourself that mis-creations form in the mind and only you can fix your perception.**

Today's Daily Affirmation is:

I am responsible for what I give this world. I choose to spread what I want to receive in return.

The actions and words that you put out into this world are the same ones you will receive back into your life. If you choose to spread anger, you will receive it. If you choose to spread love, you will receive it. If you choose to be jealous, you will receive it. Should you choose to spread wisdom, you will receive it. Choose to spread peace, and you will receive peace. Choose to spread hate, prepare to receive it.

When we question the events that happen in our lives or the circumstances we end up in, don't play the blame game. Take a second and review yourself. Look within and examine your behavior and words and actions. *What have you been doing? Have you been gossiping* – perhaps that's why others are doing it about you? *Have you been accusing others* – that's most likely why you are now in a position of being accused. Reflect on this. You are responsible for this, not anyone else. Hello pot, meet kettle.

Today's Daily Affirmation is:

I am creating a life of miracles.

I live with a miracle mindset. I live with an attitude that miracles happen every day. I live by this mindset because I've seen it in my life as well as many others time and time again.

I often tell people who are having a bad day that it could be worse – because the truth is, it could be. Doesn't mean I don't empathize or sympathize with you or your situation. Of course, I do – I too have bad days! But it could always be worse – **even when you think it just simply couldn't get any worse, it still could be worse** – but I'd much rather look at the good and say it's getting better.

That used to scare me a lot. At times, I won't lie, it still does. *Can it always be good?* I never thought so until recent years where I've reached the conclusion that this **"doom and gloom"** mindset is all in my own perception. **It's not reality, it's the reality I had created for myself** – that I kept choosing to create for myself. **Needless to say I had been mis-creating for a very long time and what I needed to do, what I've done is I've corrected my perception. I've uncreated my miscreation.** I choose to believe there's a miracle behind every corner. I choose to look for the lessons in every situation. I choose to find the good – search for the good. **Sometimes I even have to dig out the good from a pile of sh*t – but I always find it because it's always there.**

Today's Daily Affirmation is:

I am always true to myself.

Own your truth. *What does that mean exactly, right?* Own your attitude, own your style, own your personality, own your beliefs, your spirituality, your everything – own it! Own who you are! Don't falter when someone questions you. Don't hesitate or change your mind just for the sake of temporarily pleasing someone else. Don't become a chameleon due to your environment or surroundings. **Stay true to who you are, always, always, always because your light can only impact specific souls and when you dim it down...you can't reach them until you turn your light back on for them to find their way!**

Today's Daily Affirmation is:

I am moving forward no matter what!

Sometimes we just have days where we get down on ourselves. We doubt our skills or our gifts and we question our path and our purpose. You're only human, it's okay to have those days. We all have those days. **But don't let it keep you down, you hear me!** Don't let it deter you from what you set out to do. Listen to your heart and follow it, even on the bad days. Take your moment (*or your day for that matter*), feel the frustration – feel those feelings and really feel them. Then leave them there and keep going. **Use them as motivation to keep moving forward. Use these doubts, fears and frustrations as inspiration to keep going because you are needed in this world!**

Today's Daily Affirmation is:

I am relaxing and breathing to access my peace.

Finding peace during a hectic, lopsided day is not always the easiest feat. **Our instincts are to tighten up and close off when we're stressed, but as spiritual beings we should let go and relax in moments like this.** Even though I know better now, my instincts sometimes take me back to what I was used to doing. *You shut down, breakdown, clam up and freak out!* Does that really ever get you anywhere though? *No, absolutely not!*

It's important to stay mindful that when something may not be going as smoothly as you'd like, when something goes in the opposite direction of what you had planned – just go with it. *Just breathe and go with the flow.* It's difficult though because we are human, we have an ego and fortunately yet unfortunately at times we use our mouth to speak what our ego is feeling. You know how you look at the flame on a stove and you know it's hot and so you say to yourself, **"DO NOT TOUCH."** We need to train our minds to work the same way in life – in difficult situations. We need to train our minds to say, **"BREATHE, it's all going to be okay!"** We need to tell ourselves, *"Roll with it, it's not the end of the world."* When you try to teach a child to not touch a hot flame on a stove, there are some children *(not all)* that don't believe you. Some kids want to touch anyway. Some kids **DO** touch anyway and they get burned. You'd think that would stop them, but there are some people that don't learn the first time and do it again – and sometimes, *again and again and again.* **Do you find yourselves making the same mistakes again and again and again?**

Do you find yourselves going back to the same bad habits over and over and though you **KNOW** better, you aren't doing better? **STOP** and breathe. It's all going to be okay. **Let go of the mistakes, let go of the past. Forgive yourselves for not learning as quickly as you'd like. Forgive yourself because you will get it, don't worry about it – just be mindful of it.** *Slow down, be in the moment, stay present and think before reacting, responding and perceiving.* Don't you dare shut down or freak out. There's always another chance, relax and go with it!

Today's Daily Affirmation is:

I give freely and without expectation.

Give freely and without expectation. There are too many people in this world who give and expect to receive OR they don't give at all and expect to still receive. When they don't, they become resentful of helping in the first place.

Why must everything be given with expectations? Why are we unable to give and do so without an open, unexpecting heart? When you help, when you give freely of yourself, your time, your heart or what have you – understand that it doesn't matter if that person gives back to you. **Trust that the energy you are putting forth to offer yourself or your gifts to them and this world will eventually be returned to you tenfold.** *When you give, you always receive* – it might not be when you want to or how you want to or what you wanted – but you always receive somehow, someway!

Today's Daily Affirmation is:

I am trusting that what is meant for me will stay and what is not meant for me will go.

If you're holding on too tight, let it go. Release your need to control. You are not giving God the credit he deserves by holding on so tight. Let him do what he's good at. Let him intervene. **Let God be God!**

All you need to do is trust. Trust that it will be okay, because it is **ALWAYS** okay! Trust that your best interest is **ALWAYS** at hand and **that what is meant for you will stay and what is not will go.**

Today's Daily Affirmation is:

I am almost at my miracle!

You are not the only one struggling. Sometimes we feel so alone, but the truth is that people all over the world are feeling the same as you at times. **You are not alone. We are all connected; we are all one!** Stay focused on what's important – your passions, your dreams, your love. Stay focused and stay in peace.

You are not alone. **You might feel like giving up, but you receive the greatest opposition right before your big breakthrough – right before your miracle!** *Don't quit 5 minutes before your miracle.* Keep going!

Today's Daily Affirmation is:

I am full of potential.

Sometimes our spirit needs to be rejuvenated a little to realize our full potential. Just like every other human being in this world I go through hills and valleys. Days where I can't come up with anything witty to write, and I sit and struggle, and other days it flows right through me. I've realized that when I reach a day where I am struggling for the words, it's because I need to take a step back, refresh my thoughts and breathe.

We can consume ourselves with all these responsibilities and demands from day-to-day that perhaps we spread ourselves so thin that we end up hitting a minor roadblock. **There are always bumps in the road, the trick is to learn why you hit it and how you can smoothly ride around it – or maybe even bust right through it** *(though I don't suggest LITERALLY busting through any actual roadblocks while driving a motor vehicle, you feel me?!)*

What I'm getting at is when you feel like you hit a traffic light that seems to be taking forever to turn green, use that time to review, refresh and revitalize your thoughts, words and actions. *Renew your spirit!* When we hit these little roadblocks it's a good time to analyze why we need to pause – why did the Universe make that happen right then and there? *Why did God tell us to pump the brakes?* Were we being so consumed by external situations that we totally ignored our internal feelings? Were we simply paying attention to the wrong things or perhaps letting the opinions of others alter what we knew on the inside? **Use this time to check yourself. Do a gut check! Do a spirit check! Check your thoughts! You'll find something in there that will move you forward again, I promise.** If you don't have the strength to search, just ask – that's what I do. *Ask for a sign. Ask for confirmation. Ask for guidance* – you will **ALWAYS**, always, always receive it! Trust me.

Today's Daily Affirmation is:

I am free from judgment.

Some people think what I write about and post always has to do with my own personal life. This couldn't be further from the truth. I write based on what speaks to me in that moment. Sure, there are times that what's happening personally to me is the subject of the day. But I also write based on a common theme my clients may be dealing with. I write based on what I receive during meditation. During one meditation a quote about **'judgement'** spoke to me. I've had some clients that have felt down on themselves or rather feeling as if they can't do anything right.

This used to be a feeling I knew all too well. When you don't know your own worth you base your worthiness on other people's words, actions, and reactions to you. You depend on **'others'** *(whomever they are: mother, father, aunt, cousin, neighbor, boyfriend, girlfriend, husband, wife, etc.)* to build you up and when you don't feel as if **THEY** are satisfied, you tear yourself down. Take it from me – one with personal experience of this very behavior – **STOP DOING THAT!!!**

Your worth is **NOT** dependent upon if someone else likes you. Your worth does **NOT** rely on how much money you make. Your worth is **NONE** of these external factors at all! **Your worth is knowing WHO YOU ARE on the INSIDE. Knowing your spirit and your heart. Knowing your own character. Knowing it and owning it. Loving it and being proud of it.** When you don't know your own worth you feel judged, all the freaking time. You feel judged by the way you dress, eat, talk, walk, act, work, breathe. This is no way to live. Judgement will exist in this world no matter what. **If you are constantly feeling judged, I want you to look within.** Search your soul and find the reason why **YOU**; *beautiful, talented, intelligent YOU* feels that way. It doesn't matter what others think of you, it's none of your business. But if you **FEEL j**udged, that's on you. Don't attack back as most like to do. **When you stop judging others, you stop judging yourself.** You then free yourself from your own judgement and from clinging to the judgement of others.

Today's Daily Affirmation is:

I am allowing the Universe to do its job.

Allow whatever comes to come. Allow whatever goes to go. You are okay and the Universe has your back always. Stop worrying and just allow. Allow it **ALL**! Embrace it all! You need it. You deserve it. You will grow from it. You will learn from it. **It's happening FOR you not TO you and you need to just let go and allow.**

Today's Daily Affirmation is:

I am a source of powerful energy!

Energy is powerful! Everything is energy – **WE** are energy. Everything we do, say, and think is energy. **If you can grasp this concept and remember it, you can change your life.** When you fear something, you place that energy out into the world, it manifests, and what you are fearing takes place. The same if you love something, believe in yourself, hope or wish for something. This post might sound a bit fluffy but sometimes you can get the message across in a very simple way.

Try this out: Write down something, anything you want for yourself. Read what you wrote out loud and believe it has already happened. Now if you have any doubt in your mind, anything like, *"yeah right, I could never get this,"* then scribble it out and pick something new that **"seems"** more reasonable or attainable to you. Big or small, it doesn't matter. I wrote myself a check the other day. I didn't question the amount at all, I wrote down the first number that my intuition lead me to and I believed it, wholeheartedly. I hung the check right in front of me so I can see it every day when I sit at my desk. **I'm claiming what is mine from the Universe.** *I want you to do the same!* **We are not victims and we are not meant to live miserable lives full of struggle and heartache.** *Abso-freakin-lutely-NOT!*

We are rich and full of love. We are abundant in all realms and we are beautiful, blessed spirits! We can have it all, we can have every single thing we've ever hoped and dreamed of and it's just a matter of what I explain to my clients as **NOT** *"mind-f**king"* yourself. You, yes **YOU**, need to believe it in order to receive it. **I believe I will receive the amount I placed on that check.** I've done this before with so many other things. Sometimes I write them down, other times I shout them to the Universe. So write down what you want, **BELIEVE IT** *(really, truly believe it's already yours)* and make like you've already received it. Place it where you can see it and every time you look its way, know it belongs to you. *Then just sit back and watch the magic unfold!* Be sure you tell me all about it when it does, I'll be waiting!

Today's Daily Affirmation is:

I am trusting that everything is happening for my highest good.

When you feel off-balance and a bit frustrated, it's a great time to step back and relax. **Sometimes when you pull back from a situation you are able to see it more clearly.** When you're too up-close and personal with it, it can become a little blurry or jaded.

Embrace this time because as I always say, everything is happening for a reason – every single thing...even the feelings of frustration. Whatever you are going through right now in this very moment, trust and believe it's all good. **Go with the flow and stay positive as everything is happening for the highest good of all involved.**

Today's Daily Affirmation is:

I am spreading kindness everywhere I go.

Kindness is often underrated. We need to stop devaluing such simple concepts that can make such a large impact upon other people's lives and the world as a whole. A small kind gesture to a stranger could drastically alter their day. Offering and giving kindness without being asked raises the Universal vibration for the world. It's such a simple concept.

When you are kind, you raise your own personal levels of happiness. When you are kind, you are putting something positive into this world that wasn't there a minute before. When you are kind, you will receive kindness – not always immediately, but karma repaid can take place over time and it's a beautiful and amazing thing. We are all connected, we are all one, and we are meant to spread love. Fear does not exist where love does. **Where there is love, there is kindness.**

You can get upset, frustrated, disappointed, and angry but still be **kind** because these emotions only exist based on your *perception.* **If you are able to perceive the good in all** – *everybody, every situation, everything* – **then you can correct your perception rather than mis-create.** When we mis-create we lower our vibrations. When we lower those vibes we start spreading fear, doubts, worries, anxiety out into this world. Yes, we **ARE** that powerful! *When that happens, who the heck feels like being kind, understanding, or loving to anyone?* No one does – because we've created a world for ourselves where we are **PERCEIVING** the bad, rather than choosing to perceive the good. Choose good – always choose good and always be kind. You never know what someone is going through. You never know the battles people are fighting. You never know their internal struggle. You never know their situation. It's not your job to know and it's not your job to judge – it's your job to show love and be kind **DESPITE** all that. No matter what they've done, no matter who they are, and what they're going through, it's your job to be kind.

Today's Daily Affirmation is:

The Universe provides me clarity when I step back to receive it.

Sometimes things need to get stirred up, tossed around, and even a little confusing to get some clarity! Yes, you read that right – **sometimes when you toss all your mismatched socks in the air and let them land where they want, you find that one striped one you've been searching for.**

Don't even act like that's an insane idea because the truth is that we are often too close to things to see them clearly. We often over-think things and when we over-think anything, we simply make a mess of it. *I'm an over-thinker at times, you are too – don't pretend you're not.* Most people over-think something, anything once in a while and when that begins to happen my best advice to you is just **STOP**. *Step back, breathe, release, surrender, and shut up.* **The path you should take will be revealed. The truth will be revealed. You will receive clarity. I promise you will, but the hard part is shutting your mind up. Distract yourself with gratitude today and remind yourself what's meant for you will stay and what's not meant for you will leave.** If you don't believe me, ask the Universe to remove what's not meant for you, reveal the truth, and make it clear and make it un-confusing. I do this often and ***BOOM...CLARITY***!!

Today's Daily Affirmation is:

I am flowing with the current.

You ever wake up and think your day is going to go in one direction but it takes a sudden turn and now you're going somewhere else? *It happens a lot, doesn't it!* Life has a funny little way of not paying any attention to what we've already planned out in our head and kind of just doing whatever it feels like.

But guess what? **What it "feels" like doing, is what is actually meant to happen.** What you need to do is just allow it to happen. Stop placing expectations on what you wanted or what you thought you needed or think you deserve. Just **ALLOW** whatever is taking place, to take place. **You need to not fight against the current of life and rather just flow with it.** You will be more at peace and you'll find that when you toss out the 'assumptions' and 'expectations', which often stem from our ego, situations will fall together just so, and relationships will be more natural and at ease when you don't fight it.

Today's Daily Affirmation is:

I always see the light through the darkness.

The sun always shines when the clouds part. **We all go through moments of struggle or darkness. I say moments, because that's all they are.** Even if they last a few years, time doesn't exist when we speak spiritually. So they are *"moments"* because it's like chapters in a book – it may continue from chapter 5 – 7 but once those lessons are learned (*because that's all they are*) you will be **"brought out"**.

We also all go through periodic daily struggles – be it mental, emotional, or even physical. But just like a thunderstorm, the clouds always part and the sun will shine through. These lessons get stirred up to **TEACH** you something – could be patience, empathy, compassion, trust, etc. *Once you recognize the lesson...*it's time to turn the page using the lessons you just learned to step into the next chapter fuller, wiser, and happier – because THAT was their purpose for showing up anyhow.

Today's Daily Affirmation is:

I am grateful for the natural flow of miracles.

It's time you go outside, look up, and say thank you. This world is beautiful and the Universe is so magical. *What we think are tough times only feel tough because we're fighting against them rather than allowing them to flow naturally.* When we allow things to flow naturally that's when miracles happen.

Live in a miracle mindset and step away from the fear. **Fear is an illusion, and it's not real. It only pops up when it senses joy because it's job is to steal your joy.** Hold on to your joy by expressing the gratitude you have for this abundant Universe and all the magic it provides.

Today's Daily Affirmation is:

I stand confidently in my own truth.

Too many times we seek outside opinions and input for what actions we should take in our life, but realistically you already have the answers inside of you. Sure, you could argue, *"But Amy, don't you give advice for a living as a life coach?"* **No, I give guidance and offer wisdom to help clients perceive themselves as well as their situations in a different context.** I never tell a client what to do, but I do guide the client into accessing their intuition and making the best choices for their life path. *A big part of what I do is helping you tap into your intuition!* **The truth always lies within the spirit of your own being.** You can't get better **"advice"** then you can receive from your own spirit.

Do not allow the opinions or reactions of others in your life to dictate what you know is your truth. *Make this your daily mantra:* **"I can admit my faults and work to better myself, but I can also stand in my truth."** When my interactions don't go smoothly, I turn within myself first. I examine my truth, my words, and my feelings. If I can confidently stand behind what I've spoken, how I've acted, and how I feel then I don't allow myself to be swayed. But more times than not when you examine yourself **FIRST** you will realize that the reason that interaction is rocky is because your spirit is detecting you need a shift. It might be a lesson to grow you, heal you, teach you, or test you.

Don't let it deter, frustrate, or disappoint you. **These lessons and tests are happening for a reason. You need them and you need them at the exact moments they're happening.** Trust this process of life. Don't fight against it. When you fight against it, it only causes more chaos. Flow with it naturally and allow it to unfold the greater picture that will eventually become clear to you.

Today's Daily Affirmation is:

I speak to myself with love and compassion.

Your main purpose being alive is to get to know and love your inner self. That inner spirit that provides you not only with wisdom and guidance but love and support. How we converse with our inner self, reflects in our external surroundings and relationships. How we perceive it does the same. **The minute you allow the ego to flood you full of lies is the minute you become out of touch with that inner being.**

It's nearly impossible for anyone to not be overtaken with ego-minded words or feelings at times – *so I'm not about to tell you the secret to avoiding it.* But the goal is to master putting it back in its place. The trick is to recognize and identify when it's flooding your spirit with deceit and stop it right in its tracks. The only way this is possible is to build a strong foundation. **To get to know yourself and love yourself so much so that the minute the ego tries to lead the way, you will see it in your relationships and you will feel it in your spirit.** Then you can flip it immediately by simply recognizing and reminding yourself of who **YOU** really are. **Remind yourself of the love you have for your inner true being and observe how the compassionate energy you express towards yourself will be reflected in your encounters and relationships around you.**

Today's Daily Affirmation is:

I have a grateful heart.

A grateful heart opens up your life to miracles. *Did you know that the more you appreciate the things you already have in your life, the more you are blessed with even more?* It's true! *Were you aware that ungratefulness breeds negative energy, bitterness, and resentment?*

What you have right now in your life, whether you consider it "good" or "bad" – well, it's there for a reason. It's yours for a reason. Sometimes, more often than not, you don't need to know or figure out the reason it's there. **Just appreciate it and all it has to offer you, be it good or bad because it has a specific purpose in your life.** Eventually it'll all add up, make sense, and the puzzle will be pieced together as to **WHY** it was there, but until then, *just be grateful for it*. **Open up your heart to allow what is so your life can unfold into what it's meant to be.**

Today's Daily Affirmation is:

I am open to receiving what's meant for me.

Your life is full of synchronous moments: events that will all eventually make sense as to why they occurred. These events are meaningfully related. These moments however are not meant to be obsessed about. We aren't supposed to become attached to the desire to figure them out. The day will arrive that it'll click in your head, *"ohhh, that's why I had to work that random job for so long,"* or *"now I understand why that relationship ended."*

When you begin to live your life looking at things through your spiritual eyes, you stumble over many of these moments or rather...they are revealed to you more clearly. **The problem so many people often encounter is they dwell on them.** They obsess over them and try to figure out the why and the where and the how come. **My advice to you is to just let these moments be.** They are special in themselves and in a sense, dwelling on them is not hurting the actual event, but it is hindering you from being open to receiving more that, again, will eventually all make sense. But they will make sense, **THEY WILL** – *when it's their time to.* **Let them be what they are in that moment so your life can flow more easily in the direction it's meant to go.**

Today's Daily Affirmation is:

I am able to make anything happen.

We make a choice every single day. **Go make sh*t happen or don't. Doubt, dwell, sit and sulk, or get up and go with a positive mind and a smile on your face.** Here's the thing, that choice is strictly yours. That choice **SHOULD NEVER** be dictated by your circumstances. That choice should never be altered due to your emotions. **If sh*t is getting you down, it's because you've allowed it to. If you're questioning everything you know and do, it's because you've let your mind take you there.** *Enough!* *Stop destroying yourself from the inside out.*

You only know what you allow yourself to know. You only do what you allow yourself to do. You can only believe as much as you allow yourself to believe. Allow yourself to start realizing that the choice is all on you. It's up to you and only you know what you want to do and how you want to do it. We all have free will. Go after what you want and don't allow yourself to talk you out of it. **Refuse to make excuses, refuse to see the negative, refuse to get distracted by bullsh*t!** *Let's just keep it real for a second* because **all of this happening around you, it doesn't have to be the way you don't want it to be if you choose to make it the way you wish for it to be!**

Today's Daily Affirmation is:

I am right where I need to be.

Sometimes we can be so hard on ourselves to overcome or succeed. *I know I am a lot of the time.* **But we need to be gentle with ourselves and be kind to ourselves because when you feed your spirit love, it's like pumping gas into a car.** When you feed it anger, frustration, doubts, fears, and punishment, it's like driving on empty.

In no way am I saying don't get motivated, inspired, or determined to accomplish something you set out to do. I just want you to understand that as we all are always learning and growing in this life, we need to be gentle and kind because we're doing the best we can with the information we have at hand. **We're doing the best we can with how we're perceiving our life, ourselves, and our situations.** We can **ALL ALWAYS** improve. We should all **ALWAYS** be working to improve – *ourselves, our goals, dreams, relationships, careers.* **Treating yourself with compassion and kindness will actually build you more strength and stamina. It'll open you up to more knowledge with a greater flow of wisdom and intuition.** It'll help you see and understand more clearly. *Be good to you. Love yourself. Give yourself a pat on the back because you're doing just fine.* You are right where you should be and heading right where you need to go.

Today's Daily Affirmation is:

I am headed in the right direction!

Listen when you hit resistance it doesn't mean you should stop, turn around, and head in another direction. *No, absolutely not!* **When you hit a patch of resistance it just means you're heading in the right direction.** It means you're about to grow and make a breakthrough. If your ride was smooth all the time it wouldn't be exciting. **No one stands in line for a roller coaster with no loops, twists, or turns.** If the ride was smooth and straight, it'd get boring. There's nothing to learn, nothing to challenge us, help us grow, improve or excite us.

When you hit resistance in life, this is the Universe's way of saying, **"KEEP GOING, DON'T STOP NOW! YOU'RE HEADING THE RIGHT WAY!"** It's a clear-cut sign that you're about to make a leap to the next level. It might bring up some feelings, emotions, and turbulence, but don't let that stop you. Keep going; your breakthrough is there! Push through, embrace the pain that might be stirred up, feel the feelings, and don't look back. **What's on the other side of all of this is magic and beauty! Seriously, what's on the other side is THAT miracle –** that thing you've been hoping for – *that thing you've been working towards.* That lesson you kept missing but will finally learn. Everything will finally *click* when you hit the other side. *What's on the other side is exactly what you need!*

Today's Daily Affirmation is:

I am turning my attention inward to focus on the truth.

When we set an intention and turn our attention towards it, magic happens. I practice this during my morning meditations. Setting an intention to change my heartbeat and turning my attention towards it and witnessing it change. Then I expand and set different intentions within my body and turn my attention towards it and watch the magic happen.

This is exactly how our thoughts work in *"real life"*. **What we focus on, we manifest. What we turn our attention to and set an intention for – it happens.** Today I want you to set this intention, *"I move through my days light-hearted and carefree knowing all is well."* **Now turn your attention inward on your heart as you repeat this mantra in your mind or out loud. Then observe how your day unfolds!** You have nothing to lose, give it a try and watch miracles unfold!

Today's Daily Affirmation is:

I am patient.

Sometimes we need to be placed in situations in order to humble us, ground us, and teach us. Sometimes God puts us in places so we learn how to wait, have faith, and be patient. That doesn't mean we're purposely being tortured or tormented, that means we need to open up to the possibility that we can **LEARN** from the *"struggle"*. We can **ALWAYS** learn from the struggle.

Sometimes the lesson is merely to be patient. **Understand that all is happening in divine right time. Everything taking place in your life is happening exactly when it should.** Be patient and trust it will all fall into place at the right moment – *because it will!* We learn in these waiting periods and as my pastor says in church, *"Sometimes we need to be broken in order to be delivered. Doctors say where you've been broken, you always heal stronger then where you haven't."* So be patient and focus on your lesson. Trust it'll all work out with your best interest at hand and believe that you will come out stronger and wiser.

Today's Daily Affirmation is:

I am allowing life's flow to happen without judgment.

People don't always understand what it means to just "**vibe**" with the flow of life. This is how I explain it to my clients:

Picture yourself in an ocean. You're floating in the water or laying on a raft or board. As the waves roll in you just sit and allow them to flow right over you. It's peaceful. You don't fight them. Have you ever watched someone trying to get out into the ocean as the waves are breaking on them? When they walk into them, they get knocked over, turned, and usually tossed back further towards the beach. When you dive into them though and allow them to flow over you and around you, it's much easier, isn't it? Then you make it out and you float with the current. It's difficult to fight against the current in the ocean just like it makes life difficult when we fight against it. When you ebb and flow along with the current, it's a beautiful experience. There is no resistance, you just vibe.

Just as you allow the waves to roll over you, you need to allow the waves of life to roll over you. Do not judge them as **"good"** or **"bad"** just allow them in and out as they come. Experience them. Enjoy them. Grow with them. Learn from them. When you fight them and judge them we create unnecessary stress, worry, and fear. **We create things that don't actually exist. Today just flow. Today just ride the wave of what comes and what goes. Today do not judge or label anything or anyone as "good" or "bad". Today just allow. When you surrender that need to control, what's supposed to happen, happens easier and faster than it would when you try to place it in a tight little box, strap it in, and label it.**

Today's Daily Affirmation is:

I am focused on what I want.

"Thoughts precede everything" according to American author Pat Heldman. *But it's true!* **When you focus your thoughts on something, that something expands.** In Pam Grout's *E-Squared* book, that, I absolutely adore, she has you conduct an experiment using green bean seeds and an egg carton. The experiment has you basically focus love, light, and intention onto one row of the green bean seeds you plant in the carton and pretty much ignore the other row. Basically what takes place and has taken place for the millions of readers who conducted this experiment from the book – **the row that was focused on with intention sprouted and grew faster and taller than the row that was ignored.**

This is how our thoughts work. We can so easily get trapped into ego-minded thinking. This is fear-based thinking. **We project fears from our past forward onto our present events and future ones. This traps and blocks us from moving forward. We end up in a vicious cycle of events that keep resembling our past because we've pretty much created them from what has taken place in our past.** This is not healthy, but we all have done it at least a few times until we finally realize there's a lesson to be learned. Today's affirmation is simple in context – **focus on what you want and not what you don't want.** If you have trouble *(like I so often do)* mentally keeping your thoughts in check, journal them out. Write down **WHAT** you want to happen. **Write your story. Focus on it with love and intention.** Then sit back and watch it unfold!

Today's Daily Affirmation is:

I am capable of anything!

It's really quite incredible how the tiniest shift in your thoughts can make radical changes in your life. It really shouldn't surprise me since this is what I do for a living, however it never ceases to impress me. *The magic that is this Universe delivers 100% on time, all the time.* It gives in ways you can't even imagine and has quite a sense of humor about it too!

Stay in your power. Own it. Breathe it. Be it. Claim it. Know that everything is always working out for you no matter what is playing on the surface…. deep underneath; it's all being rearranged in your favor. You're always winning as long as you believe you are but that choice is yours. Do you believe you can have it all? Do you believe you are worthy? Do you believe God is FOR you? Believe it…so you can receive it!

Today's Daily Affirmation is:

I am a success.

Sometimes we are put in positions where we don't always want to do what is asked of us, but we know that if we don't at least try, no growth will take place. *And isn't growing what being alive is all about?* If we stayed stagnant from birth until death, what would be our purpose here? We wouldn't learn, experience, feel. We are meant to grow like flowers grow. **We are meant to take root, give life, expand, share and yes, sometimes we're even meant to just be what we are.**

Point is that if we want to just remain a seed in the dirt and refuse to grow, we will never see or experience the beauty that is this life. **In order to take advantage of all that is offered to us, we have to be willing to step outside our comfort zones. We have to be willing to push ourselves to limits that we might have easily just placed on ourselves.** Meaning, we are capable of *SO MUCH* and yet we hinder ourselves with fear. We hold ourselves back with insecurities, doubts, worries and fear of failure. *But how do you know you'll fail if you never actually challenge yourself to try?* It's rhetorical, don't shout your answer at this book just pay attention for one more second – **stop placing limitations on yourself and on your life.** We make the decision on how much or how little we accomplish. **WE** decide our path. *It depends solely on our thoughts – on our mindset towards ourselves.* You make the decision, so which mantra will you be repeating today: I will fail **OR** I will succeed? *(I mean, that's kind of rhetorical too as we all know it's the latter!)*

Today's Daily Affirmation is:

I choose happy.

We aren't supposed to be taking everything so seriously. Life isn't meant to be that serious. Yes, we learn lessons, we experience things that can be **"good"** or **"bad"** – based on how we perceive them, we ride the roller coaster of emotions throughout the entire thing but if you're going to take **EVERYTHING** to heart it's going to be quite a miserable ride. *Lighten up folks!* **Put a smile on your face, allow joy into your heart and just roll with the punches.**

You make the decision on what affects you and how it affects you. If you want to choose gloom and doom every single time something doesn't go as you **"expected"** it to go, *then go for it.* But be aware of the energy you're putting out because it gets returned to you. **Why not choose joy? Why not choose happy?** Why not choose to make **"bad"** situations into funny ones. *Laugh at them.* Laugh right in their face and exert the positive energy that will come back to you in different forms tenfold.

Today's Daily Affirmation is:

I am manifesting all my desires by believing, affirming, and letting go of control.

Anything you want is yours, you just need to believe it. *Now, saying you believe it and actually believing it, affirming it and holding it truthfully in your spirit are completely different things.* You need to understand what all has to work together to be able to manifest your desires.

Saying you **"believe"** and holding a *real belief* in your spirit are completely different. **When you hold it in your spirit, nothing can sway you.** Nothing anyone says, no obstacles thrown your way, nothing trying to throw you off course at all will make you question, doubt or fear. Easier said than done but when you let go of trying to control ***how*** and ***when*** it happens and just ***allow*** what you believe in to happen, that's when you have no fear any longer!

Today's Daily Affirmation is:

I am focused on my happiness.

Sometimes you need time for just you. Sometimes you need to remind yourself what makes you, you. Happiness is an inside job. It cannot be dependent on the people in your life or your circumstances. It cannot be determined by your bank account or job title. Happiness IS you. You with me?

Happiness is the pure essence of who you are. That means that it's the sh*t that makes you, you. It's the quirks that come from you and make you unique. Smile at them. Laugh at your jokes. Be with yourself. Enjoy your company. You are important. You are unique. You are extraordinary and to think that there will never EVER be another like you in this lifetime is amazingly powerful truth to realize and be happy about!

Today's Daily Affirmation is:

I am committed to truthful perception.

We live in a world with such a thin veil between perception and knowledge that even those of us who recognize this can struggle with the two. I'm going to give it to you straight though: **What happens around you is all simply a perception of what is happening.** We want to believe it's knowledge, the ego would like us to believe that, but we're just projecting memories forward into our present and future.

In order to not repeat your "past" you need to make a commitment and conscious choice to not apply what 'was' to what 'is'. *If for one second you pay attention to the ego's lie, you alter your entire perception of what is taking place – therefore manifesting that lie into reality.* **The good news is what you have created (rather, mis-created) you have the ability to un-create. The power all lies within you my dear.**

Today's Daily Affirmation is:

I am reflecting and attracting what I think and feel within.

We go through periods in life where suddenly things we've always heard make a lot more sense. Then there's times where what we *"thought"* made sense suddenly **(and I literally mean SUDDENLY)** turns the light-bulb on in our head and magic unfolds. You get a sudden **"AHA"** moment and are astounded that it clicked the way it did when you once understood it on a different level. **This, my friends, is what is better known as a 'miracle'.** *A correction in your perception.* A correction in your mind placing it back on its right-minded path.

That path is to give and receive love. That path teaches us that what we see in others, is what we see in ourselves. It's how we see ourselves. It's a mirrored reflection. Picture yourself walking into a room full of mirrors – *will you like what you see looking back at you?* If you don't, direct your attention inward and you can change what you see. The right-minded path does not include fear or worry. **This path shows you the truth in everything. This path will bring you endless love and unlimited happiness.**

Today's Daily Affirmation is:

I am tuned into my personal happiness!

Somewhere along the road of life we were taught, influenced or reached some form of a delusional conclusion that life isn't meant to be enjoyable at all. Somehow along the way we wanted to grow up so badly and yet as you do grow up, you hear a lot of adults sulking, complaining and just mucking through their days just to get by. **We were never made to just get by.** Individually we are full of power and wisdom that a lot of us have decided to just drown out and ignore. *That doesn't mean it left us though.* It's still there, you've just hidden it and covered it up with nonsense and fears.

Life isn't about how much money you make; how many degrees you earn, or the number of friends you hang out with. Life isn't about how many ridiculous photos you post on social media or how many Likes you get. **We each have a purpose.** So many go through life thinking they need to search for that purpose – *which couldn't be further from the truth.* I used to think the same thing because that's what they teach you in school. **The truth is you don't need to search for anything. Your purpose can easily be revealed to you if you just listen to your inner guidance** – *your spirit.*

Your happiness revolves around what's in your spirit. That voice is always there and available, you just need to tune into the right frequency – *the right channel, the right station!* So many don't want to listen because they're scared of what it might say. They're fearful that it might tell them what they probably already know in their gut and are ignoring. **Ignore all you want, but eventually you're going to be lead right back down the path of tuning in to that voice.** That voice is going to lead you straight to unlimited happiness. It'll bring you peace, love, wisdom and an abundantly fulfilling life!

Today's Daily Affirmation is:

I move through my day knowing everything I experience is a response to the love I have for myself.

The root of every "problem" starts with a lack of love. It begins with the idea that we are separate from everyone and everything. But this couldn't be further from the truth. **We are all connected. The idea of holism is that we have an interconnection that does not exist on its own.** For those who I might have lost – the idea of "karma" – *what goes around, comes around*. What you give, you receive. When we feel as if we are separate, we view people and situations as "bad" or "good". We get fearful and/or we feel guilt. We lash out in pain, frustration and/or anger **rather than realizing that the situations happening are those in which we've created ourselves.**

I often have people that approach me asking me to explain this better so they can grasp it. It took me a while to comprehend this as well. Many years in fact it has taken to really stronghold this idea that there is no such thing as being a victim or feeling guilty or getting punished. You rarely encounter someone who has understood this concept at a young age because we're brought up made to feel as if we're separate. **The actual concept is quite simple though: the LOVE you have for yourself is the LOVE you experience, feel and see around you – happening to you and for you.** Lack of love for yourself creates a gap in your whole-being and thus creates the idea of separation. This seeps into our relationships and experiences. So when we say "look within" it's because the minute you shift your perception of YOURSELF to yourself, that's the minute you see change on the outside (in those relationships and experiences).

Today's Daily Affirmation is:

I am rewriting my reality with positive truthful statements.

We all have the habit of repeating the same negative mantras to ourselves daily. We all have different things that we think, feel and believe about ourselves and our lives. **The problem is that the more we continue to repeat these things in our minds, the more evidence we seek out to prove they're true.** *But what if you were to change the negative to a positive?* What if you decided to take that *'thing'* you continue to tell yourself and flip it into the opposite? **For example:** "I am the worst person to talk to in the morning." ---> **New Reality:** "I am the best person to talk to in the morning."

It has already been proven over and over that our thoughts are what create our realities. The thoughts you continually tell yourself in your mind every day, all day are what you not only end up believing, but you train yourself to look for evidence to prove that statement true over and over again. **Why not train your mind to look for something different?** *Why not start confidently stating the opposite of every negative falsehood you tell yourself?* **Why not just see what happens?** I could tell you what happens, but that'd ruin the fun of writing these, now wouldn't it! Give it a go, you've got something on your mind as you're reading this – *I know you do*. Take that sentence and now tell yourself the opposite of it. Every time that phrase pops into your mind, tell yourself the opposite of what you normally say.

Today's Daily Affirmation is:

I am worthy of love because I am love.

When we hold things against others, we hold them against ourselves. So essentially the way we feel towards others is a reflection of how we feel about ourselves. I know for sure you've encountered the type of person at some point in your life who has nothing nice to say about anyone else. There's always something wrong with the way someone is doing something. **This only reflects this person's personal feelings towards him or herself.** This doesn't make them a "bad" person because as I've stated previously, we are not meant to judge anyone or anything as "good" or "bad". This just means that this person is lacking love for themselves, therefore creating a gap resulting in a separation that makes them either feel as if they are better than or worse than another human being.

Then you have individuals you encounter who are always cheering on others and lifting them up. That doesn't mean they don't have the occasional "complaint" or "frustration" that just means that the way they see others is a complete reflection of their love for themselves. *This is the type of love we're meant to have and demonstrate.* **We build ourselves up so much that it shines onto others. We know our own worth and understand that comparing is unnecessary because we are all unique and individual and special in our own right.** We each have our own gifts to offer this world and though some are often 'similar', no two are alike ever. Praise yourself today. Lift yourself up and celebrate you and all you have to offer this world. **You are divinely perfect and it's time you start recognizing that!**

Today's Daily Affirmation is:

I stay present by seeking gratitude.

Stay in the present moment and when your mind begins to wander *(which it will try, I promise you that!)* **steer it right back to the here and now by expressing gratitude for what is.** It really might feel silly at first if this is something new to you, but what I like to tell clients to do the minute they feel their mind leave the present and begin future-tripping – look at something right in front of you and express out loud, **"That's Amazing!"**

This little trick is something I personally learned from an experiment in one of Pam Grout's books. **Needless to say, even if you REALLY don't think whatever you just looked at is amazing, stating that phrase out loud shifts your mind to a state of gratitude.** It works immediately upon leaving your mouth and you can then once again leave what was where it was and what may be or will be where it could it and focus on what is right now.

Today's Daily Affirmation is:

I magnetize every single thing I need simply by acknowledging it's already mine.

I have found lately that a lot of people I speak with are focusing more on work and money rather than developing themselves, enhancing their minds, growing their relationships and following their passions. Somewhere along the way society has taught us to focus on external situations, superficiality and *we'll go there*...money. I didn't grow up lacking anything but somehow even I developed a mindset of lack along my journey feeling as if there might never be enough. Or worse...as if it'll all just run out.

Who taught me this? I have no idea. *Where did I pick this up?* No clue – but I do know that I am not the only one and though I have since focused my attention inward on what truly matters, I still encounter people daily "worried" about everything. **No one ever taught us that there will always be enough. No one ever reminded us that if we just find what we love and chase after it, we will be supported 100% every single time!** Absolutely no one...and yet this is the shift that we all need.

This tiny yet radical shift makes all the difference in our life. **This shift in perspective opens up an energetic flow in the Universe that was already there, we just blocked it with our own garbage. This flow of energy provides us with everything we need all the time.** Every single thing, *including money*, that you need will be provided to you if you simply just start believing that you are not lacking anything.

Today's Daily Affirmation is:

My love for myself reflects the love I see around me.

I know they say perfection doesn't exist, but did you know that you are perfect? Every single thing about you is perfect. Your individuality and unique qualities were given to you for a purpose. You are meant to embrace them, love them, cherish them, find the beauty in them. We aren't meant to compare or look at someone else and think, *"I want what they have."* If you were meant to have what they have, you'd be them. *But you are you!* **That means, what you have is customized just FOR YOU!**

What you have is special. Who you are is special. Some of us take years to recognize this. Some spend years questioning this. Some even go out of their way down a destructive path to prove they are something else. *This needs to stop!* The way you look, the way you laugh, the way you joke, the way you walk, the style of clothing you're drawn to, your many talents, your intelligence – **ALL** of this is specific to you. All of this is made for you. All of this is what you need to embrace.

Once you recognize that the quirks and weird habits you have are beautiful to you, you open yourself up to love on the outside. Because until you wholly love yourself for all of you, *every freakin' ounce of you*, until you do this – you have a padlock on the door to love in this life. **So unlock the door, leave it open and start embracing all that YOU are.** You are beautiful and amazing and made of love. **That means we're meant to love and be loved and what you see and experience in this world is a reflection of how you feel towards yourself**. So if you're 'searching' or 'pondering' why it's not happening – that's because you don't feel it towards yourself yet.

Today's Daily Affirmation is:

I am expecting miracles!

Expecting good things to happen in life is perfectly okay but there's a fine line between expecting and dwelling. *The goal of expectation is to expect it, release and let it go.* Give it up to God (the Universe)! You put the intention out there and now just trust that it's taken care of, because it always is.

The trouble we as humans run into (*and I know this from firsthand experience*) is we expect, hope and dwell. **We dwell, then we obsess. We want it and we want it now.** Sorry, it's not like that's impossible but typically it doesn't happen that way. **You see the energy you put out needs to be pure and honest and positive. Obsessing and dwelling on something exudes a negative energy.** This is only going to block and delay your blessing. *Don't the best things happen when we least expect them to anyhow?* Yes, you don't need to answer, I answered for you. **Yes, they do!** So take notice of the difference and if you catch yourself dwelling and obsessing I want you to stop, breathe, let it go. **The Universe always has your back. It only wants what is best for you. It may not always happen exactly how you want or when you want but it'll happen.**

Today's Daily Affirmation is:

I am willing to let anything in without deciding first whether it is good or bad.

Judgement immediately creates separation. When we label or judge another, we are making them and their feelings wrong and separating them from ourselves. But we are not separate we are all connected and intertwined as one. **So if you are judging another, essentially you are judging yourself.**

By releasing judgement, you silence your mind and move into loving acceptance of *what is* happening in this very moment. *Deepak Chopra* says, "That the need for judgement arises from the need to be isolated – this is the ego's form of defense." But at the same time, he says, "you are pulling away from your true self." **By forming judgments, we build walls that shut off the flow of spirit coming to and through us.** Today I want you to set the intention to be willing to let anything in without labeling it first. Remove any judgment of good or bad. This is part of a meditation I do every single morning. **Just allow without judgement and let the Universe maneuver you in the direction you need to flow.**

Today's Daily Affirmation is:

I am worthy of love and respect.

We are all equal, and we must exude that energy in all we do and all we say. That also means that the respect you demand needs to be the respect you give. **You shouldn't settle for anything less than what you would expect to receive.** I always say we need to see others as we see ourselves because we are all connected. Therefore, when you encounter individuals you feel are *"above"* you or *"better"* than you – this is an internal perception that needs to be reassessed.

You have created a gap in your own love for *you* that makes you feel like you lack something that someone else may have. This is where fears arise in love and relationships, career and finances, self-worth and self-love. **If you find yourself feeling unworthy of success or love or money let's say, then take a moment and reflect inward on why you have created this fear.** Perhaps somewhere along the way you felt that unless you received praise for accomplishments, you accomplished nothing. Maybe you were actually told you're not good enough. It could be a range of different things that your subconscious picked up along your life's journey, but regardless of where it came from, the way to resolve (heal) it is to provide yourself with the love and respect that you want to receive from the external world.

Today's Daily Affirmation is:

I love myself enough to know my limits.

Setting boundaries with individuals can be difficult at times especially when they choose not to understand. *You know what is best for you. You know what your spirit needs.* But it's difficult to remain on a peaceful path when others try to intrude and steal your peace out from under you. It doesn't matter who they are, what their title is or how old they may be – **you are worthy of holding on to your peace and if that means setting limits for others, that is what you need to do.**

The problem arises when others are offended by the boundaries you place on them however **you are only responsible for the energy you carry and the energy you share.** *The energy they bring is solely their responsibility.* **If they are choosing to perceive you loving yourself enough to know your limits as "bad", that is a gap they've created within themselves and it is only up to them to fill it with love by looking at you and the love you carry in a loving way rather than a harmful one.**

Today's Daily Affirmation is:

I am trusting where I'm being guided is for my highest good.

Trust your struggle. Trust your guidance. Trust your path. We are constantly being guided. It's okay if you misinterpret the messages though and end up on a wrong path. **The path you're meant to go down will still be there and you will eventually be guided back**. When you head down the wrong paths you are consistently redirected without even realizing it half the time. Things just *"don't work out"* or fall through. *You get rejected or declined.* **These blocks redirect us.**

Wonder why that relationship just didn't work out? **It's the same reason your GPS says, "recalculating."** Sometimes we're allowed to take these wrong turns to help us grow and learn. They always, always, always teach us something. That's why they say life is lived forward but understood backward. Hindsight is always 20/20 when we reflect back and realize, *"Oh, now I understand why I wasn't hired,"* or *"Now it makes sense why this friendship ended."* It will all make sense.

I want you to look at even the things that didn't work out for you the way you had planned today and shout, "Thank You!" We can't always make sense of things because some things aren't meant to be made sense of. **Just trust it; like you plug in that GPS and trust it's going to get you to the right destination – trust this process of life.** You are being looked out for and it's always for your highest good!

Today's Daily Affirmation is:

My gifts inspire others!

You are inspiring! Yes…**YOU!** *We often get into a habit of downplaying our own abilities.* I know I do this all the time. We feel as if someone else can always do it better than we can. This couldn't be further from the truth and here's why: **What you have to offer and the way you have to offer it to others is very unique. So special in fact that no one else can replicate it because only you are the one who can deliver it that particular way.**

I have a very authentic way of writing. The way I speak is the way I write. The tone, voice, language, speed is all authentic to me. I know many talented writers and amazingly wise life coaches and mentors and they have very unique gifts of their own that I cannot duplicate. *So why do we often spend so much time comparing and doubting ourselves?* **Why get upset by someone else's gifts when you have your very own that are just as beautiful?** *Praise their gifts to enhance your own!* **You see because when we can identify the beauty, talent, wisdom and love in another, we can see it in ourselves. When we see it in ourselves, it illuminates and expands.**

Today's Daily Affirmation is:

My intuition guides me towards love and light in all I do.

Listen to your intuition. It can speak to you in so many different ways through meditation, through messages, signs or symbols. **You can't fight your spirit when it speaks, especially when you've come so far along your journey to tune out the ego talk and tap into the spiritual truth.** *What is your spirit telling you to do?* Listen. *Is your body tired?* Rest. *Do you feel pushed to go somewhere?* Go.

I encourage you more than ever today to listen to its guidance. **If you don't know how here's a quick tip:** *Any internal thoughts or feelings you have that aren't linked to fear – that's your intuition.* It's usually the first voice that speaks in your mind that is always kind. When you follow your spirit; your intuition's guidance, you can never go wrong. It's only guiding you towards love and truth – only towards the people, places and experiences that will serve you!

Today's Daily Affirmation is:

I choose to perceive every situation and relationship through loving eyes.

What we see each day that we wake up only holds the value and meaning that we apply to it. *We apply it through our perception.* Our perception can be harsh at times however and affect our relationships, experiences and everything we encounter. **Once you correct your perception, what you see and experience shifts.**

We wake up and have a choice. I've told you this. We move through our day with the same choice present at all times. You see there's been many times I wake up and choose happy and choose peace and then something takes place to try to throw me off course and have me not want to lean towards peace anymore – *this is life though – this sh*t happens.* So just because we wake up and say, *"I'm going to be happy today"* doesn't mean you aren't going to encounter fumbles, mishaps, stress, dilemmas or problems. **Actually the way negativity works is the minute you choose positive, negative works harder to drag you down.** Being aware of this is key.

You can view these fumbles and problems however you wish. *I choose to perceive them as a small reminder to shift my mind back towards love.* Like setting an alarm on your phone to remind you of an appointment. I choose to perceive unexpected situations, stress or mishaps in a positive way – as a **REMINDER** for me to watch my thoughts and check myself. The perception **YOU** choose is strictly up to you. You have the same opportunity to choose whatever you wish every single day. **You can carry a loving perception with you no matter the situation and find the lesson within the problem OR you can perceive every situation that doesn't go as planned as an unfortunate one, one to drag you down, upset you, steal your joy and piss you off.** *The choice is yours.* **I choose love every single time.** It's not always easy and it doesn't always want to come naturally but that's my choice. *What's your choice?*

Today's Daily Affirmation is:

I am sharing and giving my gifts freely and lovingly.

Give. Share what's in your heart. We often hear how wonderful being a giver is but feel we need to receive in order to give or we give and expect to receive. *Not true* – give and share with everyone. *We are all connected and all one, thus when we share our hearts and offer up our gifts, we are always fully provided for and compensated.* Meaning: **We always receive what we put out.** This lesson is also often misunderstood because we feel we need to *'have'* in order to give. The definition of *'have'* can be construed to thinking it's strictly material items. *Again, not true!* **You already have everything within you.**

Yes, you are fully abundant and wise and beautiful! *This is already inside of you.* The problem is we've closed that door on the inside so we can't see it right now. **We've been peering through the wrong door. The ego-minded door. The door that makes us feel fearful and on the defensive. The door that makes us label and analyze and judge. This is not our true selves.** God doesn't judge and God gives all to all. Being that God is **IN** us, we are like God. We are meant to share and give and spread the gifts we've been given **FREELY (not for free but FREELY). Giving and sharing what you have without expectation or judgement allows others to see your true self (your spirit).** This awakens their spirit within them.

But keep in mind because this is important to note that giving freely requires an EQUAL EXCHANGE. This means that as much as it's on your heart to give...if the person refuses to receive, you cannot give. Give where it's welcome. Share with those who want the message. That's the equal exchange. I cannot help a client who doesn't choose to be helped. They need to be open and willing to receive and once they are...miracles can unfold. **This is where healing begins.** You heal your mind (the one that was peering through the fearful door) as you help others heal (their mind from fear) by merely sharing and giving openly, lovingly and freely.

Today's Daily Affirmation is:

I am choosing love in all that I do, see, think, and experience.

In order for us to see love in all situations and relationships, we must first come to realize that love is all that exists. Everything else is fear-based illusions we create with our minds. **The mind is so powerful that whatever it chooses to believe, it will perceive** – *essentially create into existence*. But the only truth is love. It takes dedication on our part either way to believe whichever we choose. *But would you rather dedicate yourself to a negative experience or a positive one?*

You really shouldn't need to think about that too long. The minute – *actually the very second* - **we choose to love, we create a radical shift in our environments**. We create a shift in what we experience and what we feel. We manifest only love, only peace, only truth. The minute you see the truth in all, your experiences and relationships will be nothing but authentically real and loving. It's just a matter of what you are **CHOOSING** to see.

Today's Daily Affirmation is:

I am enjoying this moment right now as it unfolds miracles before my eyes.

Enjoy what is unfolding right now. Enjoy it all. Every ounce of it. *These moments pass and they're so precious.* They won't return again. Each moment is a once in a lifetime moment…. appreciate it!

We often forget to cherish what is unfolding before our eyes. Sometimes it's even things we've been waiting years for. **So take a moment today, breathe it in and love it out.**

Today's Daily Affirmation is:

I am grateful for what is right now.

Look at your life in this moment. **Everything you consider good, appreciate it. Everything you consider bad, appreciate it. Everything you consider unresolved, appreciate it.** Life isn't ever going to reach a state of perfection. Life is ever-evolving and always changing.

You are always changing and always growing. **Nothing will ever stay the same, and that can be a scary concept unless you remember that changes are good.** Yes...CHANGE IS GOOD! Growth is good, and change is good, and if you can maintain the perception that everything happening is for *your benefit,* then appreciation will be natural and free-flowing in your life. **Appreciation and gratitude open the doors for so much more beauty to come into your life.**

Today's Daily Affirmation is:

I am only spreading love, for only love is real.

What we have is what we are. If you love yourself fully, you allow others to love you. If you love others fully, you allow yourself to love you and you welcome the love from another into your life. This works the other way around as well. When you can see someone else with loving eyes and not attack and not judge, you open the gates for healing. When someone "attacks" you, they are asking for healing. **So your response should always be one of love.**

So how do you apply this to your life? Simple: **If you want to be loved, love yourself. If you want to be loved, love others.** If someone appears to not act lovingly, bless them with the gift of love *(kindness, respect, appreciation)* for that is where healing begins for them. If you are able to respond lovingly, you have passed the spiritual test of healing oneself and you have spread the gift of love into another's life by showing them that only love is real.

Today's Daily Affirmation is:

I am embracing every opportunity to be a blessing whenever it's presented to me.

We are continually presented with opportunities to bless others. By blessing others, we bless ourselves. When you are given the opportunity to help another, teach another, guide, love or simply be kind – the opportunity is presented to **YOU** – specifically to **YOU** for a reason. **It's because you also NEED that blessing that you are about to offer to them.**

Whatever you are about to *'help'* them with is something you also need or need to learn. Today I want you to recognize that when you are given the opportunity to help another, calm another down, give some advice, offer a helping hand, a kind smile, a loving word, **do not turn away from the opportunity. That opportunity is not only for them, it's also for you.** You might not understand **WHY** at the time, but it will always make sense later.

Be mindful of these opportunities as they are opportunities for growth. *They're like pop quizzes for life!* When you can understand it that way, **you'll realize that this person or situation isn't being presented to you to annoy you, piss you off, frustrate you, hurt you; this person/situation is here to help you grow and they were sent to you because only you can help them grow.**

Today's Daily Affirmation is:

I am grateful for the present moment.

Being present in the moment is something that can so very easily be overlooked. Really, I mean how often are we somewhere, anywhere, where we are thinking about tomorrow, or earlier today, or next week? *How often are we out and we see everyone looking down (at their phones) rather than looking people in the eye?* How often are we staring at the clock? **How often are we planning out our weeks, hours, minutes and the present day isn't even over yet?**

Realistically we need to make plans at times – of course, but *what's the point of planning if you aren't going to enjoy the moment when it's actually happening?* I attended some close friends' weddings, and before going **I made a promise to myself that I would be in the moment.** Both were weddings I had to travel to and stay the weekend so for me that meant to be in the moment the entire weekend. So no computer and the only phone activity was to communicate with the people present at the wedding or to check on my dog at home. **The memories that now exist because of a small shift I chose to make are priceless.**

I know I break these things down to a very basic, realistic place where you can understand, use and apply it, but **being present is a powerful thing**. When you keep your mind in the moment you aren't allowing it to wander. When it doesn't wander the ego has less of a chance of manipulating your thoughts. *These things aren't basic but the key principle here is when you focus on the **NOW**, you can actually appreciate what you have.* When you focus on what is, you can be grateful for it. **Gratitude and appreciation elevate our vibrations, align them with the Universe, and open us up to miracles and blessings.** Everything is connected my loves, everything comes full circle and it all starts with that one small radical shift in you.

Today's Daily Affirmation is:

I am loving and caring for myself first and allowing the Universe to mirror my actions.

Taking care of yourself, taking time for yourself, and fulfilling your needs is something so many of us overlook on a daily basis. It needs to be done daily and yet we let work, bills, stress, and just everyday happenings interfere with the time that is so very crucial for our souls to reenergize and thrive. **You see, because everything we see and experience is a projection or reflection of our internal feelings and thoughts, caring for ourselves and taking the time to love ourselves needs to be our top priority.**

You always hear people say, *"If you can't take care of you, how will you be any good for anyone else."* It's truer than you may want to believe. **The stress you feel and the heaviness on your shoulders, that's your spirit telling you it needs some tender loving care.** We need to start paying attention to these things. **You can't give much if you aren't filling yourself up constantly.** *If you aren't leaning into joy and making yourself happy, how can you help make anyone else happy?* I too sometimes get caught up and don't realize I'm "drained" until my body starts speaking to me. I get exhausted even when I've slept well. My brain gets foggy when I try to write. This is my body's way of saying, **"Hey Amy, PAUSE for a damn second, will ya? Take today for you. Be gentle with yourself. It's time to fill up the tank again."** *Just like your car needs gas, oil, air in the tires and a tune-up – your body does too.* **When you make your health and happiness the priority above all else, you will notice a shift in all your interactions and environments.** Because the way you treat yourself will be mirrored by everything you see, feel and experience. **It's not selfish to give yourself love. It's a priority.** The love, the joy, the happiness, the peace, the strength, the abundance – that will all **MIRROR** how you are treating you. So if you want the best, treat yourself the best you can.

Today's Daily Affirmation is:

I am opening myself up to be loved by fully loving myself.

To **receive love, you must first give love.** *That love begins within you.* God/Universe/Source or as author *Pam Grout* calls it, "the Divine Buzz," **IS** love. Since we are made in its likeness, we are love. Yes, **ALL** of us. We are equally loved and just as lovable as the next guy. *Sorry if that's disappointing to some of you, but it's true.*

For us to receive love, we must believe we are loved. **Spirit (within each of us) knows we are whole and fully loved, but our ego (our human body) thinks we need to earn love and sometimes it even thinks we aren't worthy of love.** *I used to believe that.* It's the biggest lie out there. We believe these lies we tell ourselves and then we end up living them. But when we recognize the **TRUTH**, which is we don't need to accomplish something to be loved. That we don't need to be rich to be loved. That we don't need a partner to be loved. That all we need to do is acknowledge and **ACCEPT** that we are already loved – **that is when we open ourselves up to BE loved by others.** Yes, folks, that's all it takes!

Today's Daily Affirmation is:

I am calling into existence all of my hopes and dreams!

As we know, energy is everything, and everything is energy! You are part of something much bigger, and it's all unfolding before your eyes. Pretty soon the dots will start connecting, and the picture will be revealed. **What you think/speak/believe, you will create and manifest into existence.** So make sure you're only focusing on what you want to happen.

Because the Universe doesn't distinguish between good and bad for you. The Universe takes what you give it and delivers it to you. Like attracts like – whether it's positive or negative. Like I said...EVERYTHING is energy (the good AND the bad!). So put out what you wish to receive and go big because the Universe also has no limits (only your mind does).

Today's Daily Affirmation is:

I am abundant and beautiful. I recognize my worth and embrace who I am. By doing so I attract exactly who and what I need into my life.

When you begin finding yourself seeking outward approval to fulfill something on the inside, you're going about it all wrong. **Everything starts within.** You've heard me say that countless times. If you are seeking love and reassurance from another, **STOP!** That love and confidence start inside yourself. **When you learn to love who you are, that love reflects outward. It lifts you into a vibration of attracting those of the same frequency – those who will mirror that feeling you have on the inside of yourself.**

We go about this love thing all wrong sometimes. *I know I did for many years.* I thought I was just dating the wrong people because I wasn't receiving the reassurance I felt like I needed from them. Nope. **Backwards!** *I didn't love myself. I didn't recognize my worth.* **I wasn't appreciating and embracing who I was, and so I was attracting individuals who mirrored that feeling – or at least that's what I was perceiving.** They could have been giving me genuine affection and love, but I wouldn't have ever known because I wasn't feeling it inside of me – so my perception of what they did or said was one that was lacking affection, kindness, understanding, joy and love.

It's all quite simple. **There is no strange or mystical algorithm for finding pure love.** *None whatsoever.* **The right people will flock (literally FLOCK) to your side once you heal your internal feelings about yourself. How you feel about yourself is what you will see in the relationships you attract.** If your relationships are destructive or unfulfilling – *turn within.* I'm not saying every partner you'll be with will offer you pure love if you truly love yourself. No, what I'm saying is you'll have less of a chance involving yourself with the wrong ones if you work on loving yourself first.

Today's Daily Affirmation is:

My attitude of gratitude attracts more blessings to be grateful for!

An attitude of gratitude should be the **ONLY** attitude we ever have. *Impossible, you say?* Nah! **There is always something to be grateful for.** If you are reading this, you are alive – be grateful! It's not as hard as you think to find some gratitude during your day, even when you feel like you're stressed out, overwhelmed and having the worst day ever. *I used to let things like this get to me.* Now I find the gratitude in what appears to be the 'stress'. **I find something to give thanks for even if I'm running late.** Perhaps that was the Universe's way of helping me avoid a car accident. Maybe my alarm clock not going off was the divine way of allowing me to get some extra sleep that my body craved. **Everything happens for a reason. Everything has its place and its purpose. Nothing is by mistake. Nothing happens by accident.**

Life isn't always going to offer you rainbows and butterflies unless you look for them. *Request them!* **It's your choice to have dark clouds or sunshine amidst the rain.** It's all up to you.

Today's Daily Affirmation is:

I give selflessly and spread what I wish to see in the world knowing wholeheartedly it will always return to me tenfold.

I know this is quite a bold statement I'm about to make, but some of us are going about this thing called life all wrong. For some reason a lot of us were raised to think you go to school, get a good job, get married, have kids, and then the cycle repeats all over again. But what about the important stuff? *What about the deeper stuff?*

Do you honestly think we're just here to go to classes and learn some stuff – *most of which we never need or use in the real world?* Do you really think we're alive to walk around like robots, mucking through our days – coming home complaining about our bosses and our paychecks? ***Do you really think we were put here to live miserably on repeat?*** If your answer was **NO,** then you're already on the right track. There are very few of us out there that were brought up being taught something different. **We can't blame our parents, and we can't blame their parents.** *This is just a vicious cycle that has repeated through all of humanity.* **Our egos took over, and we were made to believe life = struggle.**

I hate to break it to you, but it doesn't! I love being the bearer of good news, even for all you cynics out there. No, I'm not some new age hippie who lives a delusional life of peace and love. **Let's be real – we create our struggle.** That's a fact. **We create our stress.** Another fact. **We also have the ability to create good things too you know.** We can be loving and share that love with others. We can be at peace and spread that peace. We can be kind and share that kindness. I could go on and on, but nobody has time for that, so let me get to my point. **BE what you wish to see in the world.** *I choose to be who I am and do what I do and write what I write because this is what I want to see. This is what I want to experience. This is what I want to feel.* And guess what, I do – all day long. What I want depends on nobody else. If someone thinks what I do and what I believe is ridiculous, that is a mere reflection of who they are and what they are projecting. That doesn't concern me and has nothing to do with me. **I spread what I want to be returned to me.** *I spread it selflessly, and that is what life is.* It's not about your bank account, your social status, or your job title. It's not about how many degrees you earned or what school you're attending. **It's about who YOU are on the inside, and that is the world you reflect on the outside.**

Today's Daily Affirmation is:

I am equipped with everything I need already inside me. I only need to tune in to access it.

Spirituality is not only a journey of self-discovery, but it's also a practice. I must practice my lessons I coach daily, or I cannot teach them. I practice acts of self-care and self-love. I practice leaning into joy and choosing happiness over fear. I practice mindfulness in all I do and all I say. I practice being still and trusting my inner guide. I practice gratitude and patience and being thankful for all that I have believing wholeheartedly that it's exactly what I need right now. I practice trust in God (the Universe). I practice what I preach. *That doesn't make me perfect or better than anyone else. It also doesn't mean I don't make mistakes or have moments where I let my ego get the best of me.*

I'm on a journey, and when you travel on a journey, there are always bumps in the road. Sometimes it's a tiny one, and you hop right back on track before you lose your balance. Other times you slip up for a day or two (let's relate that to a detour), but you always (**ALWAYS**) learn from it (the GPS always reroutes you!). **That's what excites me the most –when I encounter uncomfortable feelings I know that I'm about to learn and grow.** Once you fill your toolbox with your necessities for your journey, you will be able to handle bumps in the road with more peace and more ease. The tools don't make you exempt from the lessons, but they help you learn. **It's like when you have the choice of reading instructions on how to put together your piece of furniture to help make it easier or just trying to figure it out yourself. Most of us always end up referring to the instructions even when we don't want to.** *Practicing these lessons every day is like referring to the instruction manual.* They keep you in check.

The best part about ALL of this is that you are simply practicing what you wish to receive in the world you live in. You are practicing what you want to experience from others. Practice doesn't make **US** perfect because we are already perfectly made – it just helps us live in a natural, free-flowing state understanding that all that we need we already have and all that we want will come to us at the perfect moment.

Today's Daily Affirmation is:

I am thankful for my presence in this world.

Giving thanks and expressing gratitude for your life and the people in it is **supposed to be an everyday thing.** *So why do some wait until a holiday with the word "Thanks" in it to voice what they're thankful for?* **Because life seems to take over every other day of the year, that's why.** On holidays, most people are forced into stopping, taking a look around and breathing in what they've been running past on their way to the office. **But we should take notes from holidays like Christmas and Thanksgiving and even birthdays because our expressions of thanks and spirit of giving should be a 24/7, 365 day a year lifestyle.**

This is where we've gone wrong listening to our egos. We think 'life' is about work and money and bills. We think we'll always be stressed and struggling, and we sit and wait for special occasions and holidays to get present, grateful and be kind. We believe these lies we create in our heads. **But if holidays do anything for you, they should be a huge reminder of the state of mind you should carry throughout the entire year.**

I'm not necessarily the most festive person. Probably because I feel as if every day is like a holiday. That happens when you do what you love for a living. It never feels like work, and you're always at peace and filled with joy living your passion and your purpose. **So holidays for me are treated like every other day. I'm grateful, I'm happy, and I'm present.** Just be. Just be present and be yourself. Do it every day – not just on Thanksgiving, not just on Christmas or Easter or any other holiday or special occasion – be who you are and be grateful for that every single day of your life. Express it, share it, feel it on the inside. When you become totally accepting and loving towards **WHO** you are and what you stand for, your gratitude for your presence in this world will vibrate out into your interactions with others in your life. **So that awareness, that presence, and that gratitude you feel on a holiday will naturally take place every day in your life.**

Today's Daily Affirmation is:

I am living totally in the present.

Be present today because presence brings the light. Shadows of darkness only live where there is no light. *So how do we access or tune into the light when all these fearful and stressful emotions overtake us?* **We stay present.** Yes, it's that simple – you know that's what I'm good at here: **practical spirituality.** *Simplifying sh*t for you!* You are in complete control of your thoughts and therefore your emotions. Don't even try to think otherwise. That is where everything begins...in your mind.

So by staying present and just existing in the moment, you illuminate the light already within you. When you are aware of the here and now your mind can't dwell on the past or worry about the future. **Darkness thrives off these emotions of stress and fear and worry.** *This is our ego's way of isolating us.* The ego knows that once you acknowledge the fact that these "worries" do not exist because we are already well equipped with and for everything, it needs to defend itself. **So its form of defense is isolating you** – it tosses you what it feels are realistic ideas and thoughts to make you panic. *These are not realistic at all. They're delusional.* **When you're present, you are fearless.** You can exist without expectation or the need to control. You don't feel the need to push or manipulate any person or situation. When you exist in the NOW, totally in the present, watch how all that you desire unfolds in your favor before your eyes.

Today's Daily Affirmation is:

I am fully backed, supported, and protected by the Universe.

Every single thing in your life has happened or is happening for a reason. You don't need to agree, and you don't need to understand. That's actually what makes it the most exciting – not understanding the "why" but knowing that there's a purpose for it all. Now sure, your human side is going to question that statement above and be like, *"Then why does the bad stuff happen?"* I'm not going to try to explain to you *why* someone you know may have died unexpectedly or gotten hurt or put away or is ill with a disease. It's not my job or place to explain *why* that's happening, *but it is my purpose to tell you that it'll eventually make sense.*

I am not exempt from bad stuff. I too have bad days. I have things I don't necessarily want to happen, happen to me. Just because this is what I do for a living and I'm the one sitting here writing about it all for you doesn't mean I'm immune to it. *No one ever promised us that life was going to be easy. No one ever said it would all be rainbows and butterflies.* **But you can always find bad in the good just like you can find good in the bad.** You can always look for the lesson or the blessing. Maybe it's something terribly bad, or maybe it's something that's minor, but it hurt your feelings – it's all still happening for a reason. **It'll make sense later. This is what I know.** This is what I've witnessed in my life. Relationships, jobs, illness, friendships, accidents, etc. these all have a place and a purpose. If you're about to say, *"But Amy, that's not fair!"* That's your ego doing the talking. **Tap into your spirit for a second, because your spirit will say, "You're reading this RIGHT NOW at this very moment for a reason too!"** Like I say, "If you're reading this, you needed this." I'm just the messenger and so if something isn't going the way you wanted it to – the way you might have planned or hoped for – *trust it's going to unfold the way it's meant to.*

When you can simply understand that you have something always working in your favor, you will let go of the need to want to control. If you can understand that this roller coaster called life is rigged in your favor, you'll just sit back and go with the flow taking in every single freakin' second of it all! It's amazing and beautiful, and it's all happening now. Just enjoy it and don't question it loves!

Today's Daily Affirmation is:

I trust my power within.

We need to accept the fact that we are in a constant state of ebb and flow. A place of acceptance, allowance, trust, and faith. A place where we must recognize when to go, when to pause and when to let go. *Sounds so complicated doesn't it?!*

It's not. **It starts with trust.** Trust yourself. Trust the Universe – that Higher Power, Source, God. **Trust because everything is unfolding for your benefit. What happens in life is not happening TO you, it's happening FOR you.** *It's happening to help you, to guide you, to teach you, to align you with the right path and the right people.* Sometimes we question this. Sometimes we don't want to believe there's good in the world or that "good" could come of what is taking place. Sometimes we aren't sure whether we need just to wait it out, push through, or be still. *How do we find the right directions?* **Where do we access the truth?** *How do we understand where to go and why?*

Trust yourself. If you need to think about it twice, don't do it. Your inner guidance is within you for a reason. It's a gift from above. It's like that voice on the GPS, *"turn right here,"* but this voice, this is in your gut, in your mind, in your spirit. **This "voice" can merely be a feeling – a push in a certain direction. Trust it.** Don't second guess it, just trust it. It doesn't steer you wrong. This inner guidance is going to teach you when to pause and when to go. This will help you better understand this complicated puzzle called life. **You have the power, and you don't even realize it. We often think we don't, but it's right inside of us – ALL of us, equally.** We all have it. *Tap into it, listen to it, and USE IT darlings* – **it was given to you for a reason.** It's there to help you, so tune in and listen.

Today's Daily Affirmation is:

I am here. I am loved. I am able. I am present.

You are such a powerful being, and we shortchange ourselves far too often of the power we hold. We often feel helpless or worthless in situations that we **FEEL** (rather...perceive) are beyond our control.

Don't you realize that everything you experience is what you've created for yourself? **It can be changed the second you perceive it differently.** Abundance is everywhere because energy is everything. **How you feel towards yourself is what draws in certain energies into your life**. If you feel you are worthless, you will attract others who treat you the same. If you feel you are abundant and beautiful, you will attract others who feel you are the same. If you feel opportunity is everywhere, and love is within everyone (*which it is!*), you will see and experience just that in your life.

I lived the other way for a very long time. **Now I live in amazement every day at how radical shifts in my mind have created such a beautiful experience for me every second of every day.** *I used to see the bad in everything. I used to feel helpless and worthless.* But we aren't. None of us are helpless or worthless. That's your ego talking. **Your ego does that as a way to isolate you and make you feel that you aren't connected to everyone and everything in this world.** It makes you feel separate and alone. *But you aren't!* You are beautiful and abundant just like I am and you have everything you need. Be grateful for today. **Set the intention right now that you are already experiencing endless miracles that will unfold right before your eyes.**

Today's Daily Affirmation is:

I am a cheerful giver. I give selflessly with an open heart knowing I will always have more of what I put out.

Give and keep giving loves. You can't receive what you aren't willing to give. That's the way the Universe works. *It's a constant back and forth motion of giving and receiving.*

To have more of something, you must be willing to give more as well. *Don't keep score.* The Universe has it all under control. **What you put out there, you will receive back tenfold.** Trust me on this. The seeds you sow you will reap the rewards in due time – at the right divine time. Give with an open heart. Give with a kind and cheerful spirit. **Give selflessly – not because you WANT to receive, but because you want to give.**

The blessings you have were gifted to you – why aren't you able to gift them to others as well? Every day should be dedicated to giving with an open heart. **We are love and love is not about possession, it's about appreciation.** So if you appreciate and are grateful for the gifts **YOU HAVE** right now, give more and watch the miracles unfold. *Watch how you are blessed with more.*

Today's Daily Affirmation is:

I am calling forth everything I desire into my life with excitement and gratitude!

Our thoughts hold power. Our words hold power. **The power they carry gets sent out into the Universe and returned to us like a boomerang.** I talk a lot about focusing on *"what is"* in the present moment – but something we need to keep in mind is we also need to look to the future with optimism. Sometimes that's easier said than done. I had a revelation where I read something, and suddenly a memory from my childhood popped into my mind and made complete sense. *It's kind of trippy when that happens, though these days that sh*t happens to me quite often.* When I was younger and even throughout the years of growing up, there was something I repeatedly said and never really had any idea the power or magnitude the words I was speaking carried. Not until I received confirmation much later!

I used to speak and *still do*, mind you with what I like to call a **"WHEN" attitude**. I used to say things to my parents like, "When I get a lot of money I'll…." or "When I get married…" I would do this all the time for everything I said. "When I'm famous…" and then things like, "Just you wait…. when I am rich I'll buy you a boat" (LOL). Obviously my spirit knew the power of the word **WHEN** over the word **IF**. **WHEN** essentially means you're prophesying the future. You're (*as the Bible says and I'm paraphrasing here*) calling into existence the things that don't exist yet. **Apparently I was way ahead of my years which is good, because when that boat arrives, I can't wait to go for a ride!**

After this happened I sat down and wrote in my journal everything I am looking forward to have happen in my future. *I wrote it and put forth the emotion that it already exists.* This is a powerful exercise and I highly suggest you give it a try. The Universe speaks to us in creative ways and let me just say this, **WHEN everything you desire begins manifesting, I can't wait to hear all about it!**

Today's Daily Affirmation is:

I am giving my light to all who need it.

You are needed in this world. Your light – *that spirit within you* – **it's needed in this world.** I receive many emails and messages from complete strangers sharing with me their hardships and struggles. Telling me about their pain and sadness. Asking me for guidance. This is where my light is needed. This is where my spirit can offer a new perspective to others. *We are all needed for different purposes. The end result is always shared however and that is love.* We can only gain that by giving though. **We receive through extension. If you aren't willing to share it, you are depriving yourself of receiving it.**

Keep that in mind the next time you ponder something so simple as why no one ever offers to do something to help you. *Are you giving with a selfless heart? Are you giving and NOT expecting?* We know we'll receive – that doesn't necessarily mean we'll receive from the person we give to though. **We are just meant to extend ourselves without stipulations, assumptions and expectations knowing full well that the Universe will boomerang back to us what we put out there!**

Today's Daily Affirmation is:

I embrace my past with love.

When we allow ourselves to start being affected by the external world, we have begun to let our ego have more power than it should. **The ego has no power – only the power you assign to it by believing its lies.** But the ego has some shifty moves and uses past hurts to pull us away from truth, peace and happiness into its fearful way of living. If you are doing, feeling or thinking fearfully; if you are uneasy, anxious and can't obtain peace – you are living by the ego's form of perception. **When you are at peace and can maintain happiness regardless of what is going on around you, you are living in truth – spiritual truth.**

Don't misunderstand me, though. Even when you are living in truth, the ego tries to catch your attention. When this happens, don't get upset or frustrated. Recognize its attempt and view it as a sign that certain corners of your spirit still need healing. The minute you accept that is the minute you reclaim your power. **You see we have the CHOICE to give our fears power or not.** You can either believe them or not.

So what I want you to remember is that when you feel a past hurt or you "think" something may be repeating itself from your past – *recognize this is your ego.* **Recognize this is the ego's way of separating you from others. This is the ego's way of isolating you and putting you on the defense. That is not truth, and our spirit knows this – but our spirit gives us free will.** You have the choice my loves and with all my heart I want you to know to always choose love. Fear can be convincing – **VERY** convincing at times, **but always choose love.** *You will never regret it.* Something that I always remind myself of when this takes place is it's an opportunity for growth, and it's a way to heal a wound to open myself up to new blessings. **Reminding myself always that the Universe only wants me to have what brings me pure and true happiness.** It's never going to place something in your life to harm you – you are just choosing to view it that way. *Choose again...* **that is where these radical shifts that I talk so much about occur.** All you need to do in life is love your way through!

Today's Daily Affirmation is:

I accept things as they are.

When we accept things exactly as they are right now in the present moment, that is the right perception. The wrong perception is wishing things to be different than they are. *There is freedom in acceptance.* Having the wrong perception gives you the false illusion that you have control over people and situations. **You only have control over how you perceive people and situations.** If you perceive them correctly, you relinquish the idea of "control" and trust the Universe is only providing you with what is in your best interest. *Step back, breathe and let go because the Universe always has your back.*

Today's Daily Affirmation is:

I am focused on filling myself up with love so I can give and receive it back wherever I go.

Stay in touch with who you are, what you love and who you want to become and the world adjusts accordingly. *How you feel internally is always reflected externally.* I say this often, but I can't emphasize it enough. It's a minute to minute, hour to hour, day to day practice of reminding yourself of your beauty, talent and wisdom. Reminding yourself just how truly powerful and incredible you are.

You might think this could be exhausting, but it's as simple as looking in the mirror and saying, "I love you." **You can create shifts immediately in relationships and situations good or bad just by how you are feeling on the inside.** I have observed it happen to me. I wasn't feeling happy inside – I was tired and run-down and running on empty and it most definitely was being mirrored back to me in my encounters with people. I recognized it immediately and even being a life coach it's not always easy to mend it for yourself, even though you have the knowledge and the right tools to help. *When I realized my ego was trying to get the best of me that day, I took some time for just me; journaled and studied some of my books to get my mind focused back on my truth.* I then went on with my day with a clear head, and an open heart, focusing strictly on my internal feelings and every single situation then turned around immediately for the better.

Some find life overwhelming at times. I know a lot of my clients tell me this, and I used to feel the same way too. **But when you remember that a simple shift in your feelings towards YOU can alter everything around you, peace returns to your life and anxiety fades away.**

Today's Daily Affirmation is:

My positive thoughts are changing my world before my eyes!

Your subconscious does not know the difference between facts or thoughts. It merely acts to create what you think and believe that has emotion and feeling behind it. That's why the possibilities are endless when it comes to manifesting your desires. You can manifest anything you believe in. *People think it's magic – this isn't magic at all, it's science.*

It all starts in the mind and extends outward. **If you think you're in pain, you send energy into that thought and it expands and triggers a physical response in your body.** Doctors have proven time and time again that when examining the brain of a person while listening to happy music or positive words, certain parts of the brain are triggered; the same happens when listening to sad music or negative words. I used medical examples to demonstrate how your thoughts can affect you physically but this holds true for what you experience in life as well. **Whenever you have a thought about anything (true or not), you are sending energy out with it.**

So why don't you try an experiment for the next 24 hours. Every thought you have, let it be only about what you **WANT** to occur in your life. **I want you to record not only how you feel during the 24 hours but the shifts you experience in your life and relationships.** You'll be amazed at what happens!

Today's Daily Affirmation is:

I recognize that my power rests in my patience.

We often don't realize how important patience is until we act out of impatience and don't get the results we were hoping for. Patience allows your spirit to step forward revealing truth once you are willing and open to receive it. **Patience in the midst of an argument allows your mind to shift from fear to love because it is within that pause, that breath, that brief break where you just wait, that something incredible happens.** Spirit overtakes the illusions the ego is trying to project. *When we act too quickly, we usually act off our ego.* But when we wait for the right moment, the moment that we're guided to move or speak, we respond with truth and from a truthful place.

Don't you realize that every little thing that is meant for you will not pass you by. That sentence has an amazing power within it because it means that no matter what, what's yours will be yours.

Don't lose your patience if what you have been hoping or dreaming of isn't here yet. There's something you don't know yet that you need to know, to be prepared for when your desire arrives. There's someone you must still meet before it comes to pass. Nothing is out of order. *Everything is happening just as it should, on time, all the time.* **Every single thing is exactly as it should be right now at this moment.** There's amazing freedom once you accept that. So be patient. **Be patient in all things because that is where your power lies. That is where your strength awaits...in that pause before miracles take place.**

Today's Daily Affirmation is:

I choose to be the real, authentic, no-holds-barred best version of me possible!

I know we all have caught ourselves comparing what we have to the person next to us. I know it has happened if not once but at least twice (or more) in your life. It's happened in mine too. **I used to wonder why others had things that I wanted and wished for in my life but couldn't seem to obtain. I pondered if I was pretty enough and if that was the cause. Or if maybe this was just what I was meant to be – one step behind the rest.**

I truly believed these false beliefs for years. I constantly asked myself why I was working just as hard if not harder than the next guy, but they always seemed to be happier and have more money than I did. **I finally discovered one day that what I was seeing in them, I had in me.** I could access all of these things I desired if I just focused on me and pursued my truth and what brought **ME** joy. What brought them joy probably wasn't going to bring me joy. *I needed to find what made me happy.* **I needed to learn that I was able, worthy, and good enough.** I needed to realize that it isn't "them" and "me," it's "us". *We are all connected spiritually and instead of lusting after what "they" had, I should encourage them and be inspired by them.* I should be happy for their gains because they can be mine as well if I choose them. But I was choosing otherwise. **It's all our choice, and it's all in what we are choosing to perceive in our life and this world.** These days I choose to be me. **I choose to be the real, authentic me, no-holds-barred. To ONLY do what I love and ONLY do what brings ME joy.** *F*ck what other people think SHOULD make me happy, I do what in fact does make me happy.* Ever since that change in my perspective, my entire world has changed for the better.

Today's Daily Affirmation is:

I choose to see the endless possibility, wonder, and amazement everywhere I turn.

Look for the good. Seek it out. **What you look for, what you focus on, what you think about penetrates your energy field and draws it into your awareness.** It's always there; you're just opening your eyes up to it when you focus on it. It works the same the other way around – focus on the bad and the negative and I guarantee you that you will find exactly what you're seeking.

Every day you make a decision on what you are going to look for throughout that day. **You have 24 hours to experience wonder and amazement, or you have 24 hours to see everything as miserable and depressing.** *The choice is yours.* It has nothing to do with your job, financial status or upbringing. It has absolutely nothing to do with your education or who you associate with. It's simply a mindset – a choice you make every single day. **Choose good because good is everywhere, happiness is everywhere, peace is everywhere, love is everywhere.** Just choose to see it – that's all it takes.

Today's Daily Affirmation is:

I am receiving everything I need right now!

As humans we block ourselves. **We create our own fears and we don't let them go until we're ready to accept the lesson once and for all.** Sometimes we **THINK** we've accepted the lesson and mastered it only to find out that wasn't the case. **Sometimes we can even pinpoint the fear and recognize how incorrect our perception is and yet like a bad addiction, we continue to play out the same old thoughts and actions allowing that fear to live on.**

But here's the thing, when you seek out goodness in your life, you **WILL** always find it. *There are no exceptions.* **When you investigate and seek out negativity, you will find that as well.** When you believe your fears (which were self-created) you feel more fear and see more fear wherever you go. When you look at your fears and recognize they have no power over you, they dissipate into thin air.

The Universe already has everything waiting for us but if we aren't on the same frequency, we can't see it. When you're on the frequency of fear, you cannot align with your divine power and truth. **When you shift and match your vibes with the Universes' vibes, everything comes flowing to you like an endless wave of abundance.** Like attracts like, always and forever.

Today's Daily Affirmation is:

I am surrounding myself only with what inspires and excites me!

Now and then it's good to release what is no longer serving you. This could be anything from objects and belongings to friends and relationships – it doesn't matter what, but if it's no longer getting you excited and not serving your highest purpose, clear it out. **Some find this whole theory pretty harsh.** *"What, you just want me to get rid of my friends?"* As a matter of fact, yes and here's why: Unless there is something about that person that you want to learn and have in your life, clear them out. Life is ever-evolving, and the cycle never stops. *People come, and people go.* Just like we buy clothes and outgrow clothes. Styles change and styles repeat themselves.

Now, I am not telling you to read this and call up all your friends and say you can't be their friend any longer. *Absolutely not.* But sometimes we cling to things out of fear or guilt. These are self-induced and brought upon by our ego. **We should only "cling to" things and people that bring us joy and inspire us.** Things that light us up! **We should only surround ourselves with individuals that lift us up and support us.** As far as the other stuff – objects, belongings, clutter – it's the same rule of thumb. I frequently go on rampages of ridding my office and room and environment of clothes and shoes and "stuff" that I do not need or use. **If it's not something I'm consciously aware of, something that I need or use often, then it is no longer serving me.** *It would be better served elsewhere.*

And here's the most exciting part of all this – not only does clearing the sh*t out switch up the energy flow in your life and environment, but it also brings about blessings. *You see, what you give, you always receive.* If you feel you need more of something in your life, give more of that to others. You'll think this idea is silly, but when my ego begins to creep up and tell me I'm low on cash, I start handing out dollar bills with messages on them. *Oh yes doll! I write little messages from the Universe on $1 bills, and I leave them around for people in my home or even in public places.* That money always comes back tenfold. **I once handed out $3 bills and manifested $300** – that's right, everything I teach and preach I've done, give it a try. Test it out and report back!!

Today's Daily Affirmation is:

I am giving myself the love I deserve and desire.

Find it in you to take a second each day and show yourself how much you appreciate you. We're so busy sometimes giving and being there for others that we forget how important it is to show ourselves some *T.L.C.* To give ourselves the attention and affection we deserve. *How do you think you'll be able to continue giving if you don't give to yourself as well?*

You won't be able to. **It's like a car running on empty. Eventually, you need to fill up the tank.** I always tell clients; you won't be any good to anyone else unless you are good to yourself first. **So the rule of thumb is that you need to remember to always F.L.Y. – this stands for FIRST LOVE YOURSELF.** Spend time every single day doing something for you. Something you love, something you enjoy and that brings a smile to your face. Something that brightens your spirit. Something that makes you feel good. *There's plenty of time, so do it!* **The amazing part about all of this is – the love you show for yourself, will be the love others offer back to you in return.** If you are depriving yourself of love, you will see it in your outside relationships. If you keep filling yourself up, you'll notice how much love you'll receive in return!

Today's Daily Affirmation is:

I allow everything to exist how it wants.

Let go, love it out and let it fall where it may. Priceless words I once received during a morning meditation. **We all need a reminder at times to just let sh*t go. Let it be what it may. Let it fall where it wants. Let it exist exactly how it wants to in this present moment.** *Love it regardless.* Don't judge it. Remove the judgment and allow it to stand just as it is – *people, situations, arguments, relationships* – just let them be what they are. **It's so easy for our minds to take us to places of 'want' and 'why not' or 'what if'. The ego lives in those places.** *Love doesn't live there. Love lives in the present.* **So today, just let everything be exactly what it is, without judgment, labels, expectation or assumption – just let it exist in the present and accept it.** Freedom rests in doing just that.

Today's Daily Affirmation is:

I only surround myself with good vibes.

Surround yourself with those who lift you up. Immerse yourself in love for the person you want to be. I truly used to think it wasn't a big deal when I hung around people who weren't supportive of my endeavors – *boy did I learn different the more I learned about energy and intention.* **First of all, you become like the five people you spend the most time with.** So if those people don't have a quality about them that you would like to have in your life, it's time to move on. It's not a bad thing to move on either – it's called growth.

Second of all, the energies you are around impact you more than you probably realize. As I grew deeper into my true-self, I noticed myself separating further from those not emitting a similar frequency. Not because I thought I was better, but because I understood the concept of what I listed above but I could also feel the drain of their energy on mine. **When you work to place yourself into a higher vibration through positive thinking and self-love, and you work long and hard at getting yourself there, you don't need one ounce of energy that is going to try to tear you down.** *The more I grow deeper and deeper into my spiritual quest, the more I attract and magnetize those on similar wavelengths.* **But as you're getting there and to maintain a healthy balance while you are there – only surround yourself with those whose vibes bring joy.** From my hair stylist to my nail lady to even those I follow on social media – if I'm not getting a vibe that inspires me, I let it go because I know something better is waiting for me once I release what is no longer serving me.

Today's Daily Affirmation is:

I am feeling my dream become a reality.

Find the strength inside of you to persevere. **We all encounter speedbumps and even roadblocks, but be grateful for them – don't take them as something negative.** They help slow you down to learn patience. They redirect you towards something better. They demonstrate to you that divine timing is important.

You will often hear successful people talk about visualization. People who, *for lack of a better word*, have "made it" in their field of interest, say that they had that particular dream since childhood. That they never took their eyes off that vision no matter what they encountered along the journey. Visualize what you want for your life. Visualize what your desire is. Write it down in a concise yet specific way and read it twice a day. Read it and as you read it, **FEEL** yourself already having it. **Feel the emotions that would run through you as if you were already living this dream out.** Do this and keep doing this. The more you visualize it, the more you bring it into existence. *The more you do, the more you send out the energy that is necessary for that goal.*

Now, does that mean you can sit back and do nothing? *Absolutely not.* Does that mean you'll be free and clear of delays and roadblocks? *No.* **But when you have a dream, a specific heartfelt desire for your future – you can feel it in your bones and nothing, absolutely NOTHING is going to stand in between you and that dream.** No delay will deter you. No set-back will hold you back. I've been visualizing something, a dream of mine from a very young age. I didn't know I was doing it at the time, but now I know I was. My spirit knew my passion and purpose and when I opened my heart and mind long enough, I was tapped into that frequency. I never knew **HOW** I would reach this dream. I never knew when it would take place. **But it was a knowing deep in my soul that I would have it no matter what and nothing no one said or did was going to stand in the way and get in between me and my desire.** This is the kind of perseverance you need and as your life coach, I highly suggest you get to visualizing right now! **I believe in you…. now it's your turn to believe in YOU!**

Today's Daily Affirmation is:

I am fully trusting the Universe without a doubt!

Trust fully in the Universe. Trust completely in God and the divine to totally support your every need. *That's all it takes!* That's all you need to do. **Faith can be hard when you want to hold on to the worrying.** It can be difficult when you want the answers to the questions "How" and "Why" and "When." *The why is already answered dolls – it's because you are loved.* **The how and the when, well those will make sense later.** I don't just say that. They truthfully will make complete sense later. You will look back and see how all the twists and turns lined up to bring about your hopes, dreams, and desires. So today let go of the how and the when and just let the 'why' be enough!

Today's Daily Affirmation is:

I am here right now for a reason.

You are exactly where you need to be. Some of us can be so hard on ourselves and our journey that we so easily forget that the pace we are moving is the exact pace we are meant to move. **We have such a stronghold on the idea of "control" that we often forget that everything has its place and its purpose.** *Everything happens exactly when it should for us.*

We need to be gentle with ourselves and this process called life. It's a process of growth – not a process to see how much money you can make or how quickly you can pop some kids out. **We learn things as we're meant to learn them. We learn them and experience them in perfect time for our divine growth.** We can't look over at the other guy and get upset because they appear "successful" in their career. They too have things they've gone through and struggled with. Perhaps they're successful in the workplace but their home life needs some extra attention. Maybe that person you "think" has lots of money and is so happy, is actually really lonely and lost. **We can't be so quick to judge and compare. We need to be kind, not only with ourselves but with our perception of others.** *You are right where you need to be.* **If you are reading this right now, you were meant to show up here, today, at this particular time and read these very words.** It's all happening for **YOUR** benefit. It's going to provide you with something you need later on today.

This is how "life" works. You need to trust. **If you're reading this, you needed this.** This goes for **EVERY SINGLE THING** in your life. *Everything!* **That guy you randomly bumped into at the store – there was a reason. If your alarm clock went off late – there was a reason. Traffic jam on your way to work – there was a REASON.** It'll make sense later. Just know and trust and believe that you are **EXACTLY** where you need to be right now. Stop wishing your days away and just live in **THIS** moment. *This moment is all that matters.*

Today's Daily Affirmation is:

I am leaning into joy and filling myself up with love and happiness!

You matter. Your feelings matter. How you feel about yourself…it matters most of all! Find the time every single day to indulge in something that brings you joy. **Treat yourself how you want others to treat you.** I have found that on days where I have put myself last and ignored the things that bring me happiness – it reflects in all my interactions that day. There's tension and stress and yet on days where I indulge myself **FIRST,** *the love just overflows from those around me.*

This is something so many people overlook. Let me tell you a little secret dolls: We **MAKE** time for the things we want to do. We all have the same amount of time – it's simply how you manage that time. **An act of self-love can take 5 minutes if you stop and buy yourself some flowers. You don't need hours to do things that make you happy.** *If you feel like there's never enough, there will never be enough for you because that is the energy you are exuding.* If you understand the way the Universe functions then you know your **NEEDS** are always provided for.

Today's Daily Affirmation is:

I am present and I am grateful for what is in my life right now.

In this present moment, what are you grateful for? **The ego would always like us to believe, "it'll be better when…." But the only moment that is real is this moment right now.** Today…stay present. Be present with your family and friends. Be present while at work. Be present in times of stress. Be present while you smile and laugh. Take in the banter and the noise and even the silence in every moment of today. Immerse yourself in it all and be grateful for it. **It may not be exactly how you'd hoped it would be. It may not be happening how you would like it to be. But it's all happening exactly as it should.**

Today's Daily Affirmation is:

I am constantly receiving divine guidance everywhere I turn.

The Universe is always giving us directions, guidance, wisdom, hints and so on everywhere we look. I often get signs that might seem like coincidence the moments they show up but **I like to call them little blasts of love from above.** When I need some direction in part of my life, I always receive guidance from unexpected sources. Sometimes a billboard while I'm driving, other times a complete stranger just says something to me and in the context of whatever it is I'm dealing with it makes complete sense. Sometimes it can come through music or even television. **It just depends if you're eyes are open and you're paying attention**. I don't just mean being awake, I mean paying attention. Being mindful of what and who is around you. *Being mindful of the words spoken to you and the sights you see.*

When you open up to it, you literally are receiving a full set of directions to your best life and all you need to do is pay attention. The Universe is as clear and as loud as that annoying voice on your GPS, but if you keep ignoring it, it will keep recalculating to steer you back to the correct destination. If you aren't listening you might feel as if you hit roadblocks and detours far too often, and that's just the Universe's way of saying, *"Hey dude…. start listening or you're going to keep driving in circles and getting detoured until you do."* **Like I always say, there's a direct message for someone even in this little affirmation right now.**

Today's Daily Affirmation is:

I am right where I need to be. I am thankful for this moment right now.

Slow down! We are all in such a hurry, but what for? We need to understand that there is always a reason for the amount of time something takes. There is always a reason for delays, redirections and what FEEL like blocks in our life. Perhaps you're being protected from something. Maybe you're being lined up to meet a particular person. Those are just some examples but my point is that *that is how the Universe works.* **That is how God directs us and protects us.** He knows what we'll do before we do what we do.

So **SLOW DOWN**, breathe and don't rush. **The thoughts we think, the words we speak and the energy we put out are so much more powerful than you can imagine.** Staying on top of it can indeed be overwhelming but it's as easy as breathing. Distract yourself with gratitude. Try to find or create the humor in situations that don't seem humorous. **You are where you are for a reason. Whether you get there fast or have to wait, it's all for a reason.** Be grateful, stay present and don't worry about what others are doing. *God is for you, not against you.* The Universe **ALWAYS** has your back and everything happening is in **YOUR** best interest.

Today's Daily Affirmation is:

I shift my attention inward to love. I release my need to focus on anything external for happiness.

There are times I catch myself worrying. Worrying about finances and time. Worrying that I wasn't spending enough time doing my work. I've even felt *guilt creeping up on me and have had to shut it down, stop, and check back into my happy place.*

There's plenty of time and plenty of money. Time isn't real, and money is simply energy. **Our relationships with people are way more important that the things so many of us sometimes focus on.** The ego likes us to think we're separate from each other and that material items can bring us joy. *This is a lie.* **The love we share trumps all material things without a doubt.** These things do not leave with us when we leave our human body. **The only thing that is true is what's of spirit and that is love, peace, and happiness.**

It may sound like a Hallmark card, but it's the truth. **Today shift your attention to love. Focus on the people around you.** Focus your attention on your relationships. *Search for the gratitude in every interaction today and tomorrow and beyond.* **Be thankful for the love you have to give. Be grateful for the people who share in the love you have to offer.** This is your life. You decide what's important – *I'm just here to tell you that as humans we lose track of what is really important at times.* **There's no need to punish ourselves for it – but we simply need to shift our attention to what is and remember that tomorrow is never promised.** You were given today – do something amazing with this gift that you have and the beautiful gifts that reside already within your soul.

Today's Daily Affirmation is:

I am choosing to live connected to everyone and everything. I am choosing truth and truth is love.

Labels and judgment all stem from the ego. There is no good or bad, right or wrong, better than or less than. **There is only our perception of what is happening in this moment.** A lot of folks don't realize how far this actually extends. *This is EVERYTHING – every relationship and every situation in life.*

When we identify something as good or bad, we are creating separation. This or that. Them or us. He/she or I. **The ego wants separation.** *Separation is how it exists – it's how it thrives.* **Truth is from spirit and spirit knows we are all one – we are all equal and connected.** No one is better than or less than. There is no good or bad; there is only what is. **What is, exists with peace and love if we choose truth.** *If we choose separation, we create turbulence in our mind and thus in our life.* Do you want to live a simple, unaffected existence or do you want chaos and turbulence? The choice is all yours!

Today's Daily Affirmation is:

I am comforted knowing that everything happening is for my benefit.

The events in your life are happening in the order in which they're happening for a reason. There's a purpose for it all. I know you don't always believe that; you may not even believe that right now as you are reading this – *but it's true*. **Everything happens the moment we are ready.** I don't mean mentally ready; *I mean spiritually ready.* **We have to go through sh*t sometimes to learn a lesson. To realize something. To understand something. To meet someone.**

When you look back on your life at this present moment, I'm sure you can vouch for the above as you go through some of the significant and what may seem insignificant events in your life. **You'll begin to realize how the pieces fit together. You'll see how the situations add up in some crazy, miraculous way and make sense.** Find comfort in knowing that whatever it is you are going through in this current moment, whatever is on your mind, whatever you might be dealing with or struggling with – *there's a specific reason for it.* **You will know the reason one day; this I can promise you.** But, until it's revealed to you, just ride the wave of your life trusting that it's all taking place to help you – never to harm you. Sometimes it may feel like it's hurting us, but you will understand later that it was never meant for that purpose. *There was a greater purpose to that event.*

Today's Daily Affirmation is:

I speak to myself lovingly.

Go easy on yourself. **You're doing the best you can at this very moment, with the knowledge you currently have on hand.** We can be so hard on ourselves, and we can be our own worst enemies –*especially right between the ears.* So be gentle. Speak to yourself lovingly. Treat yourself with compassion and care just like you would a child. **You are okay. You are right where you need to be.** Don't punish yourself for not being further along. Don't get mad or frustrated with yourself for things you didn't figure out up until right now. You will get to where you need to be in due time. <u>Nothing is by accident.</u> Timing is always on purpose. Even when it feels like you're behind schedule, you're right on time. Even when it feels like you're a slow learner, you're not. Sh*t falls into place for us at the exact right moment to benefit us and the situation we desire in our hearts. **Timing serves the purpose of preparing us for IT and IT for us.** When you get mad at yourself for where you are in life, you only block your flow. You hit the pause button, and it never feels good. Know why it doesn't feel good – because you're judging your progress and process. Judgment isn't love. Judgment is fear. Infuse your mind with kind words allowing yourself just to flow with where the Divine wants you to go, and you will not just feel better...you will flow faster too!

Today's Daily Affirmation is:

I am speaking love, health, peace, and happiness into my life.

Sometimes we encounter situations that easily make us want to revert to our "old ways". That without even thinking we catch ourselves saying and thinking things we've worked long and hard to break out of doing. *I caught myself doing this recently as I began preparing for an upcoming vacation.* Between catching a bad cold, being busy, and then trying to pack, I allowed the stress to take over when I knew that I simply knew better. *I knew what to do, but I was so run-down and sick and tired I just didn't do it.* **I didn't meditate, I skipped my daily reading and studies and found myself to be even more drained than ever.**

How I finally recognized that I allowed myself to be whisked away by ego stressors was when I caught myself saying things I used to say all the time. *As I so kindly refer to as "Old Amy ways" rather than my true self who I've grown to be.* Instead of just showing gratitude and embracing the fact that, *"ya f*ck it...it may be inconvenient, but I'm sick, and I'm going to rest,"* **I caught myself complaining. I saw the words I would text to people and realized I was only making all this much worse than it needed to be.**

Instead of saying, *"I am feeling better today,"* I saw myself saying, *"I feel miserable."* Sure it might have been true that I did indeed feel miserable, but I knew better than to confess it. **So I changed my tune internally and started speaking what I wanted to see into existence.** *I spoke health and kindness into myself.* Low and behold I woke up feeling so much better. **I even was able to manifest $100 out of my empty wallet while packing.** You see dolls, it all starts within our mind and thoughts. *We're all susceptible to the stress and bullsh*t that happens – but do we need to soak it up?* No. Do we need to feed into it? No. **Can we reverse all of it by simply confessing something better?** Absolutely!

Today's Daily Affirmation is:

I am pushing through my fears and stepping towards my miracle.

How do you plan on growing if you don't want to change? *How do you plan on moving forward if you continue looking back?* Pertinent questions, aren't they? We hear so much about "comfort zones" and that we won't get very far unless we step out of them. *But what exactly is a comfort zone?*

It's our place of comfort. **It's that standard of living we're used to. It's that environment where we feel safe. It's that mindset we revert to because it's easy.** *But no one said life would be easy.* No one said that chasing your dreams would be a simple feat. *It'll be worth it* – that's what "they" say. **The point is if you aren't willing to step outside the box and try something different then what you're used to, you're never going to get very far.** It's going to scare you. It's going to make you nervous. It's not always going to be easy. But I promise you this...it'll be worth it. When you push through your fears, that is when miraculous things unfold in your life. Trust me.

Today's Daily Affirmation is:

I am setting a positive tone for my day by choosing positive thoughts and vibes.

You set the tone for your day. You make the decision how it's going to unfold, and the Universe merely responds to your thoughts and your energy. If you wake up with an attitude because something didn't go the way you planned, then you have the decision right then and there to flip it and accept that everything is happening exactly how it should **EVEN** if it's not happening how you'd like it to.

Your thoughts are giving the Universe the directions to where you'd like your day to head. If you keep thinking, *"This day is the worst day ever,"* the Universe responds to that because it doesn't know "good" or "bad" it just knows the intention. **So by proclaiming something negative, that energy and intention direct the Universe, and that is all you receive in return.** By confessing something positive, it works the same way – you will **ALWAYS** receive positive if you think it, feel it or confess it. *So what tone are you choosing to set for your days?* Think about it… but if you ask me…I suggest always choosing positive!

Today's Daily Affirmation is:

I am grateful for how far I've come and excited for where I'm headed.

You are very strong. **You have been paving the path of your life for quite some time now. You have guided it in the direction to where you currently are, and so the question remains – are you pleased with your decisions?** Have you guided yourself to the places you've wanted to go? *Are you at peace with where you are?*

If you aren't, the good news remains every single day that you can choose otherwise for your path. You can say no. You can redirect. You can switch it all up <u>IF</u> you want. You don't have to wait for anything or anyone else. *It's all up to you!* Pat yourself on the back for how far you've come. **Be proud and get excited for where you're headed. You have done amazing and IF you don't feel like you have, just know that everything happens for a reason. Every choice you've made thus far was for a reason.** Don't regret a single thing because it all needed to happen – the joys, the friends, the relationships, the mistakes, the victories – **every <u>SINGLE</u> thing has happened <u>FOR</u> your benefit!**

Today's Daily Affirmation is:

I am surrendering my questions and releasing my need to control. I am winning at life because the Universe has my back!

Life takes unexpected turns. We don't always understand why or know where it'll lead, but if we trust that wherever its leading us is for our best interest, then we can allow it all to unfold freely and easily. When you let the Universe and God just work in your favor – *which is all they're ever doing* – life never feels like a struggle. *There's no resistance.* **Resistance is self-induced by us because we lack trust when we listen to our egos. We think we need to handle sh*t ourselves, or it'll never get done.**

One of the biggest lessons I need to help most clients through is understanding

that it's not ALL on their shoulders. *Sure, they need take action. Yes, they can't just sit back and hope and pray for things to fall in their lap.* **BUT knowing that once you take action, you can trust things to happen the way they should – that's the secret to success.** We don't make things happen for ourselves without the help of the divine above. We work in alignment with divine guidance. Once we start walking, our **steps are being directed. Our paths are being guided, and people are being placed in our path for our benefit.** This all requires trust.

If you've felt like everything relies on you, you're lacking that secret ingredient of trust. Why not start walking and allow the Universe to lead you? I promise you won't ever regret it. I'm living, breathing proof. **The minute I let go of the "control" factor, my life just started to fly in the direction I had always hoped and dreamed.** No one needs to understand HOW things happen for you, and no one needs to know WHY they're taking place…all you need to know is that the Universe, God, that Sacred Buzz…it's on your side. *They aren't against you.* They're working for you. **Like I say, this game of life is rigged IN YOUR FAVOR! It's like playing a game you already know you're going to win at. You're going to win at this 'thing' we call life. You are going to be happy. You are going to be healthy. You are going to have every single thing you could ever hope and dream for just stop trying to make it, force it, control it, manipulate it into happening.** Just **ALLOW** it to flow. Allow it to unfold before your eyes. *I promise it'll be amazing!*

Today's Daily Affirmation is:

I magnify my power by focusing on my breath.

How do you find your strength every day to persevere? How do you keep going? Who do you turn to? Do you even turn to anyone? **Often, it's easy to feel all alone.** So often it can feel like you're in this vicious game of life as a single-player. You don't necessarily get power-ups and extra lives if you fail in the real world, *so what do you do when you feel lost, confused and alone?*

Have you ever thought about turning within? It might be the last thing on your mind when you're distraught, but it's the best option available. **Our power resides without ourselves.** Yes, there's a Universal force working in our favor at all times, but we can tap into that power immediately by turning inward. By sitting still and listening to our inner guidance. *So cliché right?* You hear it so often in spirituality and self-help. **Focus on your breath? But why? What does that even do?**

When you can remember that you are a very powerful force living within a human shell, you can understand that **ALL** that power that lives in the Universe around us….it also lives right inside of you. That power that makes the wind blow and the waves crash. That life-force energy that is omnipresent. That "thing" that exists that people refer to as God or the Universe – that very power lives inside of your soul. **You can access it when you recognize that it's there. You can access it by simply listening, and that is why you often hear "focus on your breath".** <u>Your breath brings you back to the present moment. Your breath reminds you that there is more within you than you even realize.</u> So when your day feels like it's becoming chaotic, when you feel lost and confused, when you don't know where to turn … **turn to your breath. Magnify your power within and remind yourself that YOU already have all that you need right inside of you**…it's just that human shell blurring your vision from the truth. *So turn to your breath to find that truth and I promise that you will see the light no matter what you're going through.*

Today's Daily Affirmation is:

I am creating the life I dream of by wrapping my thoughts up in love.

The secret to life is to simply follow your bliss. *What makes you happy? What brings you joy?* Do it! Do all of it. **When we continue to believe the fearful paradigm that life is miserable, full of suffering and meant to be a drag – that is exactly what we'll experience.** But there is so much amazement and beauty out there that even though I, too believed that fearful paradigm for quite some time – once I shifted my perception I was bewildered at why I didn't do it sooner.

Don't be hard on yourself if you've been living that fearful paradigm as well – just know that any day you want to wake up and choose to see the world in all its glory, you can! You can choose to see and experience anything you want in life. It's merely a choice we make every day. I started choosing joy the last few years every morning and my entire world changed. Joy is all I experienced! **I chose happy, and happiness was all I experienced. I'm not living a fairytale – this is the life I chose to create for myself, and you can do the same thing too.** It's not too late – whether you are in your 20's, like when I began my journey, or you're in your 50's and 60's. We are given a CHOICE every day we are alive. *The minute you open those eyes, you don't need to repeat yesterday.* You don't ever need to assume today will be the same as it was before. You can create something different by changing how you think. Now is as better time as any to choose something better. **Tomorrow is never promised. Make today the best day of your life!**

Today's Daily Affirmation is:

I am mindful of every encounter. I am gifted with wisdom and divine guidance everywhere I go.

It doesn't matter what you do for a living, where you've come from or where you dream about going – you have learned lessons, you have grown, you have been through sh*t and that sh*t is meant to be shared. **It needs to be shared because this life is an endless cycle of giving and receiving.** *You can't receive without sharing. You can't get without giving.*

So today I want you to remember that you are so very important. **You have power inside of you so big that you can impact the lives of so many people in this world.** You have a story to tell, and that story needs to be shared because that is what we're here to do. God made us in his likeness, and that means that although we've all gone through different stuff – we all have a united holistic purpose and that purpose is to love each other. <u>Share your knowledge and wisdom with everyone.</u> **Give to others and be open to receiving because you are worthy.** When I hopped on this spiritual journey a long time ago, there was one thing that I stayed very mindful of. That 'thing' was that I listened to everyone I encountered in life. From sitting in the kitchen with my Nana every afternoon, to a 1-minute chit chat with the mail lady – *I listened*. **The Universe speaks to us through others, and when you pay attention to their stories, you are gifted with the wisdom to help you along your journey.** The cab driver, the pharmacist behind the counter, the bank teller or the random stranger on the street – *pay attention, listen and be very mindful of the present moment.* That moment is a very precious gift from above, and you receive these gifts **<u>DAILY</u>** when you just listen.

Today's Daily Affirmation is:

I am fully supported as I fearlessly move towards my dreams.

Do you feel like you've been living or do you feel like you're standing still waiting for life to happen to you? Now that I look back, I realize that I used to stand still waiting for life to happen to me. I used to wait for the things I dreamt of just to unfold. **I was missing a crucial step – action. My faith was unwavering, but it wasn't going to work without action.** It's like having a brand new car with all the bells and whistles, but you refuse to put gas in the tank. You love the car; you believe you made a good purchase, but you can't get anywhere without the gas.

I wasn't going to get anywhere unless I made the first move. The minute I made the first step, the Universe took action – guiding me, protecting me, redirecting me if needed. I was fully supported the minute I started moving. The Universe can't help you unless you want help. It can't direct you if you're not moving. *Does a GPS give you the directions if you plug in the address but never move the car?* No, it doesn't! So if you feel like nothing is "working" for you, that's a sure sign to start moving. It doesn't matter which way you move, and it doesn't even matter if you have a clue how to begin whatever it is you're dreaming of. *Just take action.* **Start moving in that direction and I'll tell you what – God will place the right people in your path that'll help you. You will see how doors just begin opening out of nowhere and information is handed to you without you asking.** This is how the Universe works. It's just sitting and waiting for us to make a move. *The minute we do...BAM, sh*t happens that'll blow your mind.* You'll wonder why you didn't take that first step sooner.

Today's Daily Affirmation is:

I am creating the life of my dreams with my positive thoughts, words, and vibes.

THIS, right now, is real life. **The present moment is all that matters, and though it's good to "plan" for the future or even tomorrow, it's better to live in the moment.**

It's never the "end" of anything even when it appears to be coming to the end. **If you can perceive everything as a beginning, as an adventure, as a journey – then you'll realize that nothing is ever ending – it's all just the start of something amazing.** If you doubt for one second that what you desire is just not meant to happen for you – *think again* – shift those thoughts because what you think, you create dolls!

Today's Daily Affirmation is:

I am allowing my life to change and flow how it is meant to go.

Change is good. So many of us get discouraged by change. I had always been someone who dreaded any change in life. When I finally learned to embrace it, I experienced radical shifts in my life. **Change needs to occur as part of the evolution of life.** It's part of the cycle of giving and receiving. This is how we grow and evolve – by giving and receiving and embracing ALL the change that occurs in our lives.

The secret to handling change is learning never to label it as "good" or "bad". *There is never good or bad, there just is.* Labeling and judgment stem from our ego. **By placing a label on it, we make it something it's not. We separate it from its true existence – thus separating ourselves from our true existence.** As Deepak Chopra says, "when you learn not to judge, you are basically saying, 'I am willing to let anything in without deciding first whether it is good or bad.'" So by understanding that all change is always happening for your good, and it's never happening to harm you – you will align yourself with the Universal flow of life. *By accepting what is, rather than judging what is, you don't create roadblocks for yourself.* When you freely and easily accept change, your life just seems to go smoothly and everything just lines up just the way it should.

Today's Daily Affirmation is:

I can relax knowing everything is as it should be.

Doors are opening for you, but are you paying attention? Mindfulness is a daily practice. **Being in tune to the present moment and aware of synchronicities is an extremely powerful way of receiving divine guidance every day.** There is such comfort in knowing you have heavenly support no matter where you are.

When I was on vacation, I thought I was going to lose focus on my daily practices. I thought I'd be so caught up that I'd forget to meditate or notice divine signs. *Boy, was I wrong!* Whether I was at the airport, the beach, in the hotel, or in a cab – I think I was receiving more signs than ever because I was getting hit from all angles. Repeating numbers, feathers, messages, synchronicities, and even déjà vu! **It's funny what happens when you awaken – you receive minute by minute guidance by simply opening your ears and eyes.**

Being out of my daily routine taught me something incredible, though, and that's just to relax. Sometimes I panic I won't have enough time in my day to accomplish every little practice that fills my soul and by doing so, I create stress and worry in my environment. But while I was away, I had no choice but just to go with the flow and take advantage of little moments that presented themselves to meditate or write or read. **I didn't have to stress about my "routine" because God has a way of making everything work out just the way it should.** I could live in the moment and be present and still be able to do my spiritual practices knowing I was fully supported in doing so. I trusted that if the time wasn't there to read as I would normally do, that it was meant to be that way. I knew when a cab randomly drove by with the phone number being "999-9999" that it was a specific sign for me in that moment. I knew that as I explored national parks and beautiful beaches that when a butterfly or bird or a feather appeared out of nowhere that everything was as it should be. **You don't have to look hard for comfort and support dolls. It's presenting itself to you all day long, the question is, are you willing to see it?**

Today's Daily Affirmation is:

I am leaving the how and when up to the Universe.

Questioning life's happenings is something that comes fairly easy to us humans. We ask why and when and what if. We ask how and where. We inquire about all the major "W"'s and does it get us anywhere? *No, it doesn't.*

Whatever happened to trust? Why don't we just allow everything to be the way it is? **Why do we struggle to accept that everything happening is supposed to happen?** Because we believe our ego's lies, that's why. We believe that we're separate from our spirit, and we have to do this thing called "life" all on our own. *So we begin to doubt and question everything.* We begin to wonder, "What if I did this instead of this...what would have happened." Listen darling – we do have free will, but life is happening **FOR** us. Not to us. The events that take place are helping to align you with your destiny. **They're setting you up and placing you in the right position to reap your harvest, to receive your blessing! So stop questioning and just allow what's happening to happen. Leave the W's up to the Universe and just ride the wave.**

Acknowledgments

For some profound and magical reason, I woke up one day and said to myself, *"I'm going to start writing an affirmation a day on my blog... every single day."* Usually I wouldn't make such a large commitment but little did I know it would change my days, my mindset, my energy, my life, and the lives of thousands, if not more, of others who were reading them on every platform from my blog. I never missed a day.

I would receive messages daily from complete strangers telling me how my affirmations were providing them strength, wisdom, and guidance in their own lives and before I knew it, that small commitment that I made to myself at the beginning of 2014 to help me put what I learned each day into perspective, began changing the lives of not only myself but others all over the world.

Then I got the bright idea to place them all in a book. Having an "idea" for a book is one thing. Piecing the whole thing together is a task that could not have been done so smoothly without Michael Zosh and her amazing and meticulous guidance, edits, and encouragement. I can't thank you enough for your presence, light, and unwavering support of my coaching, writing, and wisdom.

To God, my Dewey, Mom, Dad, Roxanne, and Nadej, thank you a million times over for your presence, love, strength, support, guidance, wisdom, loyalty, faith, and trust when I was weak, sad, lost, confused, hopeless, torn, tormented, hurt, and scared. You were all my strength when I was weak and have always been there. Thank you from the bottom of my heart.

And to every reader of my blog and these affirmations since 2014, thank you. Thank you for your messages letting me know how they impacted your life. Thank you for reminding me that my light is needed in a way I could never even fathom until today. Thank you for messaging a stranger and for telling me how amazing my words were and how my insight, metaphors, and phrases all helped you understand things so much easier and be able to see the light of day. Thank you for showing up and reading them every day. Words can change lives and you reminded me that mine have.

Author's Note

I hope this book reminded you that life is the projection screen of your heart and your love will flow wherever you look if you allow it to.

It is this I pray that you take away with you:

You are never alone.
You are always free.
This life is what you choose it to be.

Until we meet again dear one know that these words will carry you through every single day and night you need them to.

I love you.

If you'd like to work with Amy or receive more wisdom, you can do so at AMYTHELIFECOACH.COM.

Made in the USA
San Bernardino, CA
30 August 2016